Mistaken Identities

You thrive on

mistaken

identity

Mistaken Identities

Essay
Abigail Solomon-Godeau

Curators
Abigail Solomon-Godeau
and
Constance Lewallen

University Art Museum   University of California   Santa Barbara, USA

Published in cooperation with / Herausgegeben in Zusammenarbeit mit

Museum Folkwang, Essen, Germany
Forum Stadtpark, Graz, Austria
Neues Museum Weserburg Bremen im Forum Langenstrasse, Bremen, Germany
Louisiana Museum of Modern Art, Humlebaek, Denmark

Distributed by University of Washington Press
Seattle and London

Exhibition Itinerary

November 11–December 20, 1992
University Art Museum
Santa Barbara, California, USA

February 11–March 31, 1993
Museum Folkwang
Essen, Germany

April 29–May 30, 1993
Forum Stadtpark
Graz, Austria

June 6–August 18, 1993
Neues Museum Weserburg Bremen
im Forum Langenstrasse
Bremen, Germany

September 17–November 14, 1993
Louisiana Museum of Modern Art
Humlebaek, Denmark

The Santa Barbara showing of the exhibition, its accompanying educational programs, and the catalogue were funded in part by: the Academic Senate (UCSB); the Interdisciplinary Humanities Center (UCSB); the Peter Norton Family Foundation; the Arts Partnership Grants Project, a Program of the Santa Barbara County Arts Commission, using funds provided by the County of Santa Barbara, the City of Santa Barbara and the California Arts Council; the University Museum Council; the British Council; and the California Arts Council.

Editor: Dan Meinwald

Translator: Wilfried Prantner

Designers: Bollinger, Peters & Brush, Santa Barbara, California

Printed in an edition of 3,500 by Haagen Printing, Santa Barbara, California

Cover: Glenn Ligon, *Baldwin # 4 (Identity Would Seem...)*, 1992 Cat. no. 10 Photo: Anthony Peres

Frontispiece: Barbara Kruger, *Untitled (You Thrive on Mistaken Identity)*, silver gelatin print 60 x 40", 1981 [not in exhibition] Collection Mathias Brunner, Zurich, Courtesy of Mary Boone Gallery, New York

LIBRARY OF CONGRESS CATALOGING-IN-PUBLICATION DATA

Mistaken Identities/Curators Constance Lewallen and Abigail Solomon-Godeau; with an essay by Abigail Solomon-Godeau
p. cm.

"Catalogue of an exhibition held November 11–December 20, 1992, University Art Museum, Santa Barbara; February 11–March 31, 1993, Museum Folkwang, Essen, Germany; April 29–May 30, 1993, Forum Stadtpark, Graz, Austria; June 6–August 18, 1993, Neues Museum Weserburg Bremen im Forum Langenstrasse, Bremen, Germany; September 17–November 14, 1993, Louisiana Museum of Modern Art, Humlebaek, Denmark"—T.p. verso.

Includes bibliographical references.
ISBN 0-942006-23-2

1. Minorities in art—Exhibitions. 2. Ethnic art—United States—Exhibition. 3. Art, Modern—20th century—United States—Exhibitions. I. Lewallen, Constance. II. Solomon-Godeau, Abigail. III. University of California, Santa Barbara. University Art Museum. IV. Museum Folkwang Essen. V. Forum Stadtpark.
N6537.5M57   1992
704' .03'00973--dc20   92-43801
                                                        CIP

Lenders / Leihgeber

Bill Arning and Patrick Owens

Josh Baer Gallery, New York

The Bohen Foundation

Roy Boyd Gallery, Santa Monica

Jimmie Durham

Connie Hatch

Susan and Michael Hort Collection

Nicole Klagsbrun Gallery, New York

Glenn Ligon

Yong Soon Min

Tania Modleski

Museum of Contemporary Art, Chicago

Postmasters Gallery, New York

P.P.O.W., New York

Max Protetch Gallery, New York

Armando Rascón

Lorna Simpson

Rubell Family Collections

Mitra Tabrizian and Andy Golding

Mrs. Charles Ullman

University Art Museum, Berkeley

John Weber Gallery, New York

Pat Ward Williams

Catherine Woodard and Nelson Blitz, Jr.

Table of Contents / Inhalt

Foreword and Acknowledgments

Mistaken Identities is a watershed project for the University Art Museum. Presenting the exhibition has allowed us to participate in a campus-wide effort to engage critically with multiculturalist debates. It has challenged us to confront the complicated yet pressing need to make the museum a site for active discussion and even contestation, instead of passive reflection and contemplation. And it has enabled us to question our own institutional mandate by testing the strength of our commitment to a policy of inclusion. In so doing it has also opened the door for on- and off-campus collaboration with many who share the goal of rethinking, re-examining, and broadening the relationships between art institutions and their communities. *Mistaken Identities* has made the value of outreach programs especially compelling, since the issues of identity addressed by artists in the exhibition are clearly comparable to those affecting the lives of people residing in Santa Barbara and Southern California (and elsewhere in America and abroad). The project has thus afforded the opportunity to build a bridge between artists—historically excluded, silenced, or marginalized— and a diverse public that was invited to look, to listen and, perhaps most important to our political goals, to respond.

The decision to open *Mistaken Identities* in Santa Barbara had its genesis in discussions about a major interdisciplinary conference to be held at the University of California, Santa Barbara, in November 1992 called "Translating Cultures: The Future of Multiculturalism?" Its co-organizers, Avery Gordon and Christopher Newfield, agreed that an exhibition exploring issues of cultural difference or questions about identity could contribute directly to the conference's goals and objectives. *Mistaken Identities*, which Abigail Solomon-Godeau and Constance Lewallen had been developing for a European audience, was a particularly appropriate project for the University Art Museum, since it was conceived to participate in the political discourse surrounding multiculturalism. We are grateful to both guest curators for organizing the exhibition to fit a tight schedule and for working with us so closely and collaboratively. The entire staff has gained from the intellectual rigor of their curatorial vision

Vorwort und Danksagung

Mistaken Identities markiert einen Wendepunkt für das University Art Museum. Die Ausstellung gab uns die Gelegenheit, direkt an einer Campus-übergreifenden kritischen Auseinandersetzung mit multikulturalistischen Fragestellungen mitzuwirken. Sie hat uns herausgefordert, uns der schwierigen, aber drängenden Aufgabe zu stellen, das Museum zu einem Ort aktiver Diskussion, ja sogar der Infragestellung anstatt bloß passiver Betrachtung und Reflexion zu machen. Und sie hat uns in die Lage versetzt, die Substanz unseres institutionellen Mandats durch Überprüfung unseres Engagements für eine Politik der Einbeziehung zu hinterfragen. Damit hat sie auch die Tür geöffnet für die inner- wie außeruniversitäre Zusammenarbeit mit vielen, die das Ziel teilen, die Beziehung zwischen Kunstinstitution und Gemeinschaft neu zu überdenken, zu überprüfen und auszuweiten. *Mistaken Identities* hat den Wert und die Notwendigkeit von Programmen zur Erreichung eines breiteren Publikums besonders eindringlich sichtbar gemacht, da die von den Künstlern in der Ausstellung behandelten Identitätsprobleme durchaus mit jenen vergleichbar sind, die im Leben der Menschen in Santa Barbara und Südkalifornien (wie auch anderswo in Amerika oder in Übersee) wirksam sind. Das Projekt bot so Gelegenheit, eine Brücke zu schlagen zwischen den historisch ausgeschlossenen, zum Schweigen verurteilten, marginalisierten Künstlern und einer vielfältigen Öffentlichkeit, die eingeladen war zu schauen, zu hören und—was für unsere politischen Ziele vielleicht am wichtigsten war—zu reagieren.

Die Präsentation von *Mistaken Identities* in Santa Barbara geht zurück auf Diskussionen über eine große interdisziplinäre Konferenz mit dem Titel "Translating Cultures: The Future of Multiculturalism?", die im November 1992 an der University of California, Santa Barbara, geplant war. Die Organisatoren der Konferenz, Avery Gordon und Christopher Newfield, teilten die Auffassung, daß eine Ausstellung, die sich mit kultureller Differenz oder Fragen der Identität beschäftigte, zu den Zielen der Konferenz direkt beitragen würde. *Mistaken Identities*, ein Projekt, das Abigail Solomon-Godeau und Constance Lewallen für ein europäisches Publikum entwickelt hatten, war für das University Art Museum besonders geeignet, da es als Beitrag zum politischen Diskurs rund um den Multikulturalismus konzipiert war. Wir danken beiden Gast-Kuratorinnen für die Organisation der Ausstellung, die einem dicht gedrängten Zeitplan folgen mußte, sowie für die enge und gute

and from their personal and political commitment to investigating the complexities of identity. We also thank Solomon-Godeau for her carefully crafted and well-argued essay, which provides both an insightful introduction to the exhibition's theoretical framework and a series of brilliant readings of the artists' works.

Support for *Mistaken Identities* has come from many organizations we would like to acknowledge warmly: the Academic Senate (UCSB); the Interdisciplinary Humanities Center (UCSB); the Peter Norton Family Foundation; the Arts Partnership Grants Project, a Program of the Santa Barbara County Arts Commission, using funds provided by the County of Santa Barbara, the City of Santa Barbara, and the California Arts Council; the University Museum Council; the British Council; and the California Arts Council.

We are delighted to collaborate with our distinguished European colleagues: Ute Eskildsen of the Museum Folkwang in Essen, Germany; Christine Frisinghelli of Forum Stadtpark in Graz, Austria; Peter Friese of the Neues Museum Weserburg Bremen im Forum Langenstrasse in Bremen, Germany; and Helle Crenzien, Louisiana Museum of Modern Art in Humlebaek, Denmark. Given the recent explosion of right-wing extremism, particularly in Germany but also elsewhere in Eastern Europe, the issues *Mistaken Identities* addresses and confronts have particular resonance for a European audience, and we are very pleased that this thoughtful and thought-provoking exhibition will be shown widely.

The University Art Museum wishes to thank, with gratitude, the many lenders to the exhibition: Bill Arning and Patrick Owens; Josh Baer Gallery, New York; The Bohen Foundation; Roy Boyd Gallery, Santa Monica; Jimmie Durham; Connie Hatch; Susan and Michael Hort Collection; Nicole Klagsbrun Gallery, New York; Glenn Ligon; Yong Soon Min; Tania Modleski; Museum of Contemporary Art, Chicago; Postmasters Gallery, New York; P.P.O.W., New York; Max Protetch Gallery, New York; Armando Rascón; Lorna Simpson; Rubell Family Collections; Mitra Tabrizian and Andy Golding; Mrs. Charles Ullman; University Art Museum/Pacific Film Archive, University of California, Berkeley; John Weber Gallery, New York; Pat Ward Williams; and Catherine Woodard and Nelson Blitz, Jr.

The completion of an exhibition project such as this one, with an ambitious set of outreach programs and strategies, required the cooperation and contributions of

Zusammenarbeit mit uns. Der gesamte Mitarbeiterstab hat von der intellektuellen Strenge ihrer kuratorischen Vision und von dem sowohl persönlichen als auch politischen Engagement, mit dem sie die Komplexitäten der Identität erkundet haben, profitiert. Wir danken Solomon-Godeau darüberhinaus für ihren sorgfältig geschriebenen und genau argumentierenden Essay, der sowohl eine einsichtsreiche Einführung in den theoretischen Hintergrund der Ausstellung als auch eine Reihe brillanter Interpretationen der gezeigten Werke liefert.

Unterstützung für *Mistaken Identities* kam von vielen Organisationen, bei denen wir uns bedanken möchten: dem Academic Senate (UCSB); dem Interdisciplinary Humanities Center (UCSB); der Peter Norton Family Foundation; dem Arts Partnership Grants Project, einem Programm der Santa Barbara Arts Commission, deren Mittel vom County of Santa Barbara, der Stadt Santa Barbara und dem California Arts Council bereitgestellt werden; dem University Museum Council; dem British Council; und dem California Arts Council.

Es ist uns eine Freude, mit unseren renommierten europäischen Kollegen zusammenzuarbeiten: Ute Eskildsen vom Folkwang Museum in Essen, Deutschland; Christine Frisinghelli vom Forum Stadtpark in Graz, Österreich; Peter Friese vom Neuen Museum Weserburg Bremen im Forum Langenstrasse, Bremen, Deutschland, und Helle Crenzien vom Louisiana Museum of Modern Art in Humlebaek, Dänemark. Angesichts des jüngsten Ausbruchs von Rechtsextremismus und Neo-Nazismus in Deutschland und anderswo in Osteuropa sollten die Fragen, die *Mistaken Identities* aufwirft und behandelt, für europäische Betrachter einen besonderen Nachklang haben, und wir sind sehr froh, daß diese gedankenvolle und zum Denken anregende Ausstellung an vielen Orten gezeigt werden wird.

Das University Art Museum möchte sich bei den vielen Leihgebern der Ausstellung bedanken: Bill Arning und Patrick Owens; Josh Baer Gallery, New York; The Bohen Foundation; Roy Boyd Gallery, Santa Monica; Jimmie Durham; Connie Hatch; Susan and Michael Hort; Nicole Klagsbrun Gallery, New York; Glenn Ligon; Yong Soon Min; Tania Modleski; Museum of Contemporary Art, Chicago; Postmasters Gallery, New York; P.P.O.W., New York; Max Protetch Gallery, New York; Armando Rascón; Lorna Simpson; Rubell Family Collections; Mitra Tabrizian and Andy Golding; Mrs. Charles Ullmann; University Art Museum/Pacific Film Archive, University of California, Berkeley; John Weber Gallery, New York; Pat Ward Williams; und Catherine Woodward und Nelson Blitz, Jr.

Die Durchführung eines solchen Ausstellungprojekts— mit solch ehrgeizigen Programmen und Strategien zur Erreichung eines breiteren Publikums—benötigte die Mitarbeit und die

many individuals. We were fortunate that the Santa Barbara Contemporary Arts Forum was simultaneously hosting a thematically related exhibition, *Counterweight: Alienation, Assimilation, Resistance.* Our institutions worked together in planning, funding, and hosting two educational programs. I am grateful to Nancy Doll, Director of the Contemporary Arts Forum, for being such a valuable colleague as well as a wonderful friend. We convened an advisory committee of individuals in the community and on campus to help us shape outreach and programs, and we owe that group of dedicated volunteers our very sincere thanks for making our efforts truly collaborative. Avery Gordon deserves special recognition for her advice and assistance, especially in actively involving students in the Museum's programs. I also thank Constance Lewallen and Mary Sabbatino for their suggestions about the exhibition's tour, Melissa Marsted for her help with fundraising, and Harry Reese for enlisting his art studio students to help us with promotional materials, resulting in the exhibition flyer designed by Saam Gabbay.

The entire Museum staff has done an outstanding job on a project requiring careful planning and complicated negotiations: Elizabeth A. Brown, the Museum's new Curator, who joined our team late in the project yet helped enthusiastically, effectively, and crucially with all aspects of its realization; Brian Parshall, Curatorial Assistant, who carefully tracked the exhibition's development and worked extensively on the catalog, including collating the artists' biographies/bibliographies, all with an enviable equanimity; Sandra Rushing, Registrar, who very efficiently and ably handled the specifics and complications of loans, shipping, and the exhibition's tour; Paul Prince, Exhibitions Designer, who, as always, designed the show with astute sensitivity to the curators' conceptual and aesthetic goals and with respect for the artists' work; Rollin Fortier, Preparator, who assisted with the installation and made valuable contributions to its excellence; Corinne Gillet-Horowitz, Education Curator, who effectively developed an engaging tour program for children and adults, making the challenging subject matter of the exhibition accessible and relevant; Judy McKee, Administrative Assistant, who handled all financial and other logistical matters with care and concern that exceeded efficiency; Sharon Major, Public Relations Coordinator, who developed new and creative ways of promoting the exhibition both on- and off-campus; and Gary Todd, Office Manager, who responsibly handled a range of word-processing and other clerical

Beiträge zahlreicher Einzelpersonen. Wir hatten das Glück, daß das Santa Barbara Contemporary Arts Forum gleichzeitig eine thematisch verwandte Ausstellung, *Counterweight: Alienation, Assimilation, Resistence,* zeigte. Unsere Institutionen arbeiteten zusammen in der Planung, Finanzierung und Ausrichtung zweier museumspädagogischer Programme. Nancy Doll, der Direktorin des Contemporary Arts Forum, danke ich, daß sie nicht nur eine solch wertvolle Kollegin sondern auch eine gute Freundin war. Wir stellten ein Beratungskomitee von Personen aus der Stadtgemeinde und der Universität zusammen, um uns bei der Gestaltung der Zusatzprogramme zu helfen, und wir schulden dieser engagierten Gruppe freiwilliger Mitarbeiter unseren aufrichtigsten Dank dafür, daß sie unsere Anstrengungen zu einer wirklichen Gemeinschaftsarbeit werden ließ. Besondere Anerkennung gebührt Avery Gordon für ihren Rat und ihre Mithilfe, vor allem bei der aktiven Einbeziehung von Studenten in die Museumsprogramme. Ich danke auch Constance Lewallen und Mary Sabbatino für ihre Vorschläge zur Ausstellungstour, Melissa Marsted für ihre Hilfe bei der Beschaffung von Geldmitteln und Harry Reese für die Rekrutierung seiner Kunststudenten zur Gestaltung von Werbematerial, woraus das Ausstellungs-Flugblatt von Saam Gabbay hervor ging.

Die gesamte Museumsbelegschaft hat Außergewöhnliches für ein Projekt geleistet, das sorgfältige Planung und komplizierte Verhandlungen erforderte: Elizabeth A. Brown, die neue Kuratorin des Museums, die erst zum Team stieß, als das Projekt schon weit fortgeschritten war, und doch enthusiastisch, effektiv und entscheidend zu allen Aspekten seiner Realisation beitrug; Brian Parshall, der Assistenzkurator, der die Entwicklung der Ausstellung aufmerksam verfolgte und intensiv am Katalog mitarbeitete, für den er u.a. die Künstlerbiographien/-bibliographien zusammenstellte, mit beneidenswerter Ruhe; Sandra Rushing, Archiv und Organisation, die sehr effektiv und gekonnt die komplizierten Details der Leihgaben und des Transports abwickelte; Paul Prince, der Ausstellungsgestalter, der die Ausstellung wie immer mit großem Einfühlungsvermögen für die konzeptuellen und ästhetischen Vorstellungen der Kuratorinnen und Achtung für die Werke der Künstler/innen gestaltete; Rollin Fortier, Aufbau und Aufbereitung, der bei der Installation der Ausstellung assistierte und viel dazu beitrug, daß sie so exzellent wurde; Corinne Gillet-Horowitz, Museumspädagogin, die eine einnehmende Führung für Kinder und Erwachsene entwickelte, die den schwierigen Gegenstand der Ausstellung zugänglich und relevant macht; Judy McKee, Verwaltungsassistentin, die sämtliche Finanzfragen und anderen logistischen Angelegenheiten mit einer Sorgfalt und einem Engagement erledigte, die bloße Effizienz übersteigen; Sharon Major, Pressereferentin, die neue und kreative

activities crucial to the project's completion. Skillful contributors to the catalog's production are: Dan Meinwald, Editor; Wilfried Prantner, Translator; Anthony Peres, Photographer; and Gary Bollinger and Ginny Brush of Bollinger, Peters & Brush, who designed the book with a perceptive and inspired response to the project's intellectual and artistic content and objectives. Final thanks to Laurence Rickels, Wolf Kittler, and Gisela Kommerell for their generous help with the proofing of the German translation.

Marla C. Berns
Director, University Art Museum, Santa Barbara

Möglichkeiten entwickelte, sowohl auf dem Campus wie auch außerhalb für die Ausstellung zu werben; und Gary Todd, Büroleiter, der gewissenhaft Massen an Textverarbeitung und andere Büroarbeiten erledigte, die für das Projekt unabdingbar waren. Kompetente Mitarbeiter an der Herstellung des Katalogs waren Dan Meinwald, Redakteur, Antony Peres, Fotograf, Wilfried Prantner, Übersetzer, und Gary Bollinger und Ginny Brush von Bollinger, Peters, & Brush, deren Buchgestaltung scharfsichtig und inspiriert auf die intellektuellen und künstlerischen Inhalte und Zielsetzungen des Projekts eingeht. Schließlich gebührt Laurence Rickels, Wolf Kittler und Gisela Kommerell Dank für ihre großzügige Hilfe beim Korrekturlesen und mit der deutschen Übersetzung.

Marla C. Berns
Direktorin, University Art Museum, Santa Barbara

Preface

Although *Mistaken Identities* has been nearly three years in the organizing, this catalog essay was begun in July of 1992 in Santa Barbara, only a few months after the cataclysms of Los Angeles, two hours away, and the ongoing catastrophes in Somalia and in Bosnia. Given the fact that the exhibition is concerned with issues of identity—racial, ethnic, cultural, sexual—it would be both critically and politically myopic to reflect on such art in isolation from the urgent and convulsive history that is both *out there*—two hours away, an ocean away—and *in there*, in the art, in the formation of the respective artists, in our own practices as curators and critics.

When it was first conceived, *Mistaken Identities* was intended to be a European exhibition, that is, an exhibition of (mostly) American artists *for* a European audience. As a transplanted New Yorker, an art critic living in Paris, my relations to both the emerging "discourse on Europe" and to the French art world were those of an outsider: equivocal, refracted, abstract. More pointedly, while in the United States a complex and sustained debate around identity encompassed feminism, race relations, gay rights, ethnicity, and multiculturalism, in France such debates were not only relatively recent, but curiously circumscribed. Issues of identity were usually articulated around the ostensibly concrete and material fact of the resident North African—the Other within. Alternatively, one could observe a heightened and worried attention to the meaning of "Frenchness" in response to the prospect of an economically and politically united Europe. Bracketed on the one hand by the xenophobia and racism so profitably exploited by Le Pen and the Front Nationale, and on the other by the largely token attempts to counter them on the part of the Socialist government, it hardly seems surprising that France's most recent response to the now-inescapable realities of cultural, ethnic, and racial difference is the attempt legally to establish French as the official language of the French nation.[1]

In 1990, therefore, it seemed propitious to organize a group exhibition of artists whose work, however diverse, could be said to explore various aspects of identity, the common denominator being that in none of these

Vorwort

Zwar ist *Mistaken Identities* schon seit fast drei Jahren in Planung, aber dieser Katalogtext wurde im Juli 1992 in Santa Barbara begonnen, wenige Monate nach den Unruhen im zwei Stunden entfernten Los Angeles und während der immer noch andauernden Katastrophen in Somalia und Bosnien. Angesichts dessen, daß sich die Ausstellung mit Fragen der rassischen, ethnischen, kulturellen und sexuellen Identität beschäftigt, wäre es vom kritischen wie vom politischen Standpunkt aus gesehen kurzsichtig, diese Kunst isoliert von den drängenden und erschütternden historischen Ereignissen zu betrachten, die sowohl *da draußen*— zwei Stunden entfernt, einen Ozean entfernt—stattfinden als auch *da drinnen*, in der Kunst, in der Formation der jeweiligen Künstler/innen, in unserer eigenen Praxis als Kurator/inn/en und Kritiker/innen.

In der ursprünglichen Planung sollte *Mistaken Identities* eine europäische Ausstellung werden, d.h. eine Ausstellung (großteils) amerikanischer Künstler/innen für ein europäisches Publikum. Als verpflanzte New Yorkerin, als in Paris lebende Kunstkritikerin, hatte ich sowohl zum entstehenden "Europadiskurs" als auch zur französischen Kunstwelt die Beziehung einer Außenseiterin: zwiespältig, gebrochen, abstrakt. Um auf den Punkt zu kommen: Während es in den Vereinigten Staaten eine komplexe und seit langem geführte Identitätsdebatte gab, die Feminismus, Rassenbeziehungen, Homosexuellenrechte, ethnische Zugehörigkeit und Multikulturalismus umfaßt, waren solche Debatten in Frankreich nicht nur relativ neu, sondern auch seltsam eingegrenzt. Identitätsfragen wurden meist im Zusammenhang mit dem scheinbar konkreten und materiellen Faktum der ansässigen Nordafrikaner—dem Anderen im Inneren—diskutiert. Andererseits konnte man ein verstärktes sorgenvolles Augenmerk für das "Französische" beobachten—als Reaktion auf die Aussicht eines wirtschaftlich und politisch vereinten Europa. Umklammert auf der einen Seite durch die Xenophobie und den Rassismus, die LePen und sein Front National so erfolgreich ausschlachten, und auf der anderen Seite durch die weitestgehend alibihaften Gegenmaßnahmen der sozialistischen Regierung ist die jüngste Antwort Frankreichs auf die heute unausweichlichen Realitäten kultureller, ethnischer und rassischer Differenz kaum mehr überraschend: der Versuch einer gesetzlichen Verankerung des Französischen als der offiziellen Sprache der französischen Nation.[1]

works was identity posited as unified, self-evident, or unproblematic. A secondary consideration was to bring the work of what might earlier have been dubbed "minority" American artists into a European context.

This seems still a legitimate enterprise, but in 1992, from the vantage point of California, the political and aesthetic imperatives of such a project seem even more compelling. Southern California provides an especially vivid instance of a global "borderlands" that explodes the exclusionary model of culture that high art has historically fostered. In Los Angeles, for example, there are now 83 languages spoken. This alone suggests that in our postcolonial, diasporic, postindustrial, and postmodern society, diversity and difference proliferate even as the global village contracts, even as consumerism—the dominant ideology of the West—attempts to efface and eradicate it. That L.A. has figured as the quintessential postmodern city, or that it is often considered to be an emerging art world capital is thus less significant than its demographic status as a crucible of diverse cultures, races, languages—new identities in the making.

Nevertheless, for two white women to have organized an exhibition on the theme of identity, and to have "framed" it within the terms of multiculturalism is not without a certain awkwardness. Furthermore, the catalog essay—a second act of "framing" the exhibition—is mine and cannot but represent the voice of a white feminist academic whose interpretive strategies are doubtless vulnerable on many fronts. But whatever the problems of such an enterprise, it is surely more useful to enter the breach than to take one's whiteness, or one's privilege, as an excuse to occupy the sidelines in one of the most compelling issues we confront in the present. Furthermore, the criticism that art world feminists—even socialist feminists—have been willfully blind to differences beyond sexual difference urgently requires redress. Mitra Tabrizian's comment, cited in the following essay— "racism is a problem for *white* people"—also applies here, reminding us that the malignancies of racism, sexism, homophobia, and xenophobia are not "their" issues, but ours.

* * *

Throughout the planning of this exhibition Connie Lewallen and I were greatly helped by many people. Working with Marla C. Berns (Director) and Elizabeth A. Brown (Curator) has been a great pleasure and has made this exhibition a truly collective enterprise.

Es schien 1990 also angebracht, eine Gruppenausstellung mit Künstlern zu organisieren, deren Arbeiten, so unterschiedlich sie auch sonst sein mochten, sich mit verschiedenen Aspekten der Identität beschäftigen—mit dem gemeinsamen Nenner, daß keine dieser Arbeiten Identität als etwas Einheitliches, Selbstverständliches oder Unproblematisches behandelt. Eine weitere Überlegung war, Arbeiten von—wie man das früher genannt hätte—amerikanischen "Minderheiten"-Künstlern in einem europäischen Kontext zu zeigen.

Das scheint immer noch ein legitimes Unterfangen. Nur daß 1992—von Kalifornien aus gesehen—die politische und ästhetische Notwendigkeit eines solchen Projekts umso zwingender erscheint. Südkalifornien stellt ein besonders lebhaftes Beispiel für ein globales "Grenzland" dar, welches das von der Hochkunst traditionell gepflegte exklusive Kulturmodell sprengt. In Los Angeles werden heute 83 Sprachen gesprochen. Das allein zeigt schon, daß sich in unserer postkolonialen, diasporischen, postindustriellen und postmodernen Gesellschaft Vielfalt und Differenz ausbreiten, auch wenn das globale Dorf enger wird, auch wenn der Konsumismus— die beherrschende Ideologie des Westens—sie einzuebnen und auszulöschen versucht. Daß L.A. als Inbegriff der postmodernen Stadt figuriert hat oder daß es häufig als die kommende Hauptstadt der Kunstwelt gesehen wird, ist somit weniger bezeichnend als sein demographischer Status als Brutkasten für diverse Kulturen, Rassen, Sprachen—die Entstehung neuer Identitäten.

Es mag allerdings etwas seltsam anmuten, daß eine Ausstellung zum Thema Identität von zwei weißen Frauen organisiert wurde, die sie auch in einen multikulturellen "Rahmen" gestellt haben. Zudem stammt auch der Katalogtext—ein weiterer Akt der "Rahmung"—von mir und kann nur die Stimme einer weißen feministischen Akademikerin repräsentieren, deren Interpretationsstrategien sicherlich von vielen Seiten verwundbar sind. Aber welche Probleme das auch mit sich bringen mag, es ist zweifellos sinnvoller, sich in die Bresche zu werfen, als das eigene Weißsein—oder die privilegierte Position—als Ausrede dafür zu verwenden, bei einer der drängendsten Fragen der Gegenwart am Rande zu stehen. Darüberhinaus verlangt der Vorwurf, daß sich die Feministinnen im Kunstbetrieb—selbst die sozialistischen—blind stellen gegenüber jeder Differenz außer der sexuellen, dringend nach Wiedergutmachung. Mitra Tabrizians im folgenden Aufsatz zitierter Kommentar, "Rassismus ist ein Problem für *Weiße*", gilt auch hier; er erinnert uns daran, daß die Bösartigkeiten von Rassismus, Sexismus, Homophobie und Fremdenangst nicht "ihre" Sache sind, sondern die unsere.

* * *

Während der gesamten Ausstellungsplanung wurden Connie Lewallen und ich von vielen Leuten tatkräftig unterstützt.

Brian Parshall, Curatorial Assistant, has helped us at every stage of the project; his efficiency, patience, and organizational skills have been invaluable, both for the catalog and the exhibition.

The other staff of the University Art Museum— Rollin Fortier, Preparator; Corinne Gillet-Horowitz, Education Curator; Sharon Major, Public Relations Coordinator; Judy McKee, Administrative Assistant; Paul Prince, Exhibitions Designer *extraordinaire*; Sandra Rushing, Registrar; and Gary Todd, Office Manager— have been wonderful to work with. We greatly appreciate all their efforts on behalf of *Mistaken Identities*. Dan Meinwald was an able and resourceful editor on the catalog.

Several individuals deserve our special thanks: Mary Sabbatino, Director of Galerie Lelong in New York, who helped with funding sources and gave us good counsel and suggestions; Lawrence Rinder, Curator of Contemporary Art, University Art Museum, Berkeley, who was extremely helpful in selecting the tapes of Theresa Hak Kyung Cha; and Robert R. Riley, Curator of Media Arts, San Francisco Museum of Modern Art, who gave advice on the video program in the early stages of the exhibition's development.

Connie Lewallen and I also wish to acknowledge those who facilitated the process of securing loans and information: Lisa Calden at the University Art Museum, Berkeley; Don Wheeler, Ruth Phaneuf, and Nicole Klagsbrun at Nicole Klagsbrun Gallery, New York; Nola Mariano at Circuit Network, San Francisco; Richard Telles, Director, and Jody Zellen at Roy Boyd Gallery, Santa Monica; Magdalena Sawon, Director, Postmasters Gallery, New York; Lawrence Shopmaker, former Director, Molly Sullivan, and Josie Brown at Max Protetch Gallery, New York; Kathleen Merrill, Assistant Curator at The Bohen Foundation, New York; Wendy Wood and Rachel Levin at John Weber Gallery, New York; Debby Scott Klein, Associate Registrar at the Museum of Contemporary Art, Chicago; Desi del Valle at Frameline, San Francisco; Anna Kustera at Josh Baer Gallery, New York; Scott Catto, Director, P.P.O.W., New York; and artists Jimmie Durham, Connie Hatch, Glenn Ligon, Yong Soon Min, Adrian Piper, Armando Rascón, Martha Rosler, Mitra Tabrizian, Carrie Mae Weems, and Pat Ward Williams.

Last but hardly least, I want to thank Professor Avery Gordon, Sociology Department, University of

Die Arbeit mit Marla C. Berns (Direktorin) und Elizabeth A. Brown (Kuratorin) war ein großes Vergnügen und hat diese Ausstellung zu einer wahrhaft kollektiven Unternehmung gemacht. Brian Parshall, der Assistenzkurator, hat uns in jedem Stadium des Projekts geholfen; seine Effizienz, Geduld und organisatorischen Fähigkeiten waren für Katalog wie Ausstellung von unschätzbarem Wert.

Die anderen Bediensteten des University Art Museum— Rollin Fortier, Vorbereitung; Corinne Gillett-Horowitz, Museumspädagogin; Sharon Major, Pressereferentin; Judy McKee, Verwaltungsassistentin; Paul Prince, Ausstellungsgestalter *extraordinaire*; Sandra Rushing, Archivarin; und Gary Todd, Büroleiter—waren alle wundervoll in der Zusammenarbeit. Wir wissen all ihre Bemühungen für *Mistaken Identities* sehr zu schätzen. Dan Meinwald war ein fähiger und findiger Redakteur des Katalogs.

Mehreren Personen gebührt unser spezieller Dank: Mary Sabbatino, Leiterin der Galerie Lelong in New York, die uns bei der Suche nach Finanzierungsquellen half und wertvolle Ratschläge gab; Lawrence Rinder, Kurator für zeitgenössische Kunst am University Art Museum von Berkeley, der äußerst hilfreich war bei der Auswahl der Videobänder von Theresa Hak Kyung Cha; und Robert R. Riley, Kurator für Medienkunst am San Francisco Museum of Modern Art, der uns in den Anfangsstadien der Ausstellung in bezug auf die Video-Sektion beriet.

Connie Lewallen und ich möchten auch all jenen danken, die uns bei der Beschaffung von Leihgaben und Informationen behilflich waren: Lisa Calden am University Art Museum, Berkeley; Don Wheeler, Ruth Phaneuf und Nicole Klagsbrun von der Nicole Klagsbrun Gallery, New York; Nola Mariano von Circuit Network, San Francisco; Richard Telles, Leiter, und Jody Zellen von der Roy Boyd Gallery, Santa Monica; Magdalena Sawon, Leiterin der Postmasters Gallery, New York; Lawrence Shopmaker, ehemaliger Leiter, Molly Sullivan und Josie Brown von der Max Protetch Gallery, New York; Kathleen Merrill, Assistenzkuratorin an der Bohen Foundation, New York; Wendy Wood und Rachel Levin von der John Weber Gallery, New York; Debby Scott Klein, Assistenzarchivarin am Museum of Contemporary Art, Chicago; Desi del Valle von Frameline, San Francisco; Anna Kustera von der Josh Baer Gallery, New York; Scott Catto, Leiter von P.P.O.W., New York; sowie den Künstler/innen Jimmie Durham, Connie Hatch, Glenn Ligon, Yong Soon Min, Adrian Piper, Armando Rascón, Martha Rosler, Mitra Tabrizian, Carrie Mae Weems und Pat Ward Williams.

Last but not least möchte ich Professor Avery Gordon vom Sociology Department der University of California in Santa Barbara danken, deren intellektuelle Beiträge zum Katalog-Essay

California, Santa Barbara, whose intellectual contributions to the catalog essay, including bibliographic and editorial input, have been invaluable.

Abigail Solomon-Godeau
Co-curator

[1] It is significant that the most sustained and strenuous opposition to this intensified mobilization of racism and xenophobia was of grass roots, rather than governmental origin. I refer to the formation of S.O.S. Racisme in the 1980s.

einschließlich bibliographischer und redaktioneller Ratschläge von unschätzbarem Wert waren.

Abigail Solomon-Godeau
Ko-Kuratorin

[1]Bezeichnenderweise ist die beharrlichste und aktivste Opposition gegen diese zunehmende Mobilisierung von Rassismus und Fremdenangst außerparlamentarischen Ursprungs und geht nicht von der Regierung aus. Ich meine die Formierung von *S.O.S. Racisme* in den 80er Jahren.

Introduction

"Make no mistake about it," recent U.S. presidents have been fond of saying, thereby signaling their iron resolve regarding issues of policy. Such assurances, or threats, tend to mask the complexity of crises that might be better resolved by clarity than by bullying rhetoric. *Mistaken Identities* takes as its subject one of the most difficult problems being played out on the world stage. The tragic events taking place in post-Cold War Europe and Africa demonstrate the profundity of the conflicts that arise around issues of cultural and ethnic identity. In the United States, the ideal of the melting pot has not been realized, as many ethnic and racial groups, by choice or exclusion, remain outside American culture. (What defines American culture is, in itself, a thorny question.)

The word "mistaken," as it is used in the title of this exhibition, signals an investigative rather than dogmatic approach to the issue on the part of the participating artists. Representing diverse backgrounds and modes of artistic expression, these artists address various aspects of identity—personal and social, psychic and political—as members of groups designated as racially, ethnically, culturally, or sexually "different," and explore the meanings of these differences.

That this exhibition is organized in cooperation with the Museum Folkwang in Essen, Germany, the Forum Stadtpark in Graz, Austria, the Neues Museum Weserburg Bremen im Forum Langenstrasse in Bremen, Germany, and the Louisiana Museum of Modern Art in Denmark, speaks of its equal relevance to current European struggles over the issue of national identity and to debates on the subject of multiculturalism in the United States. The exhibition's premier presentation at the University of California, Santa Barbara, has special significance as a dramatic visual pendant to the coincident interdisciplinary conference, "Translating Cultures: The Future of Multiculturalism?"

Constance Lewallen
Co-curator

Einleitung

"Make no mistake about it" ("Daß das ja nicht verkannt wird") lautet ein von den U. S. -Präsidenten der letzten Zeit gern gebrauchter Ausdruck, um ihren eisernen Entschluß in politischen Fragen zu signalisieren. Solcherlei Versicherungen—oder Drohungen—sind dazu angetan, die Komplexität von Krisen zu maskieren, die man vielleicht besser durch Klärung als durch einschüchternde Rhetorik lösen würde. *Mistaken Identities* hat sich eines der größten gegenwärtig auf der Weltbühne ausgetragenen Probleme zum Gegenstand gewählt. Die tragischen Ereignisse in Europa und Afrika nach Ende des Kalten Krieges zeigen wie fundamental die Konflikte sind, die rund um Probleme der kulturellen und ethnischen Identität aufbrechen. In den Vereinigten Staaten wurde das Ideal des Schmelztiegels nicht verwirklicht, insofern viele ethnische und rassische Gruppen, sei es aus eigenem Entschluß oder durch Ausgrenzung, weiter außerhalb der gängigen Begriffe der amerikanischen Kultur bleiben (wobei die Frage, was die amerikanische Kultur definiert, eine dornige Frage für sich ist).

Das Wort "mistaken"—"verkannt", wie es im Titel dieser Ausstellung verwendet wird, verweist auf eine eher investigative als dogmatische Behandlung des Problems seitens der teilnehmenden Künstler/innen. Unterschiedlicher Herkunft und unterschiedliche künstlerische Ausdrucksformen repräsentierend behandeln diese Künstler/innen verschiedene Aspekte von Identität—persönliche und soziale, psychische und polititische als Angehörige von Gruppen, die als rassisch, ethnisch, kulturell oder geschlechtlich "anders" eingestuft werden—sowie die Bedeutung dieser Arten des Andersseins, dieser Differenzen.

Die Organisation dieser Ausstellung in Zusammenarbeit mit dem Folkwang Museum in Essen, Deutschland, dem Forum Stadtpark in Graz, Österreich, dem Neues Museum Weserburg Bremen im Forum Langenstrasse, Bremen, Deutschland, und dem Louisiana Museum of Modern Art in Dänemark zeugt von ihrer Relevanz für die gegenwärtigen europäischen Auseinandersetzungen über Fragen der nationalen Identität im Gefolge der Auflösung der Sowjetunion. Ebenso relevant ist die Ausstellung aber auch für die inneramerikanischen Debatten über Multikulturalismus: Ihrer Erstpräsentation an der University of California in Santa Barbara kommt besondere Bedeutung zu als eindrucksvolles visuelles Pendant zur gleichzeitig stattfindenden interdisziplinären Konferenz "Translating Cultures: The Future of Multiculturalism?"

Constance Lewallen
Co-Kuratorin

Fig. 1
Jimmie Durham
New Clear Family, 1989
Cat. no. 2

Mistaken Identities
Abigail Solomon-Godeau

The movement for change is a changing movement, changing itself, demasculinizing itself, de-Westernizing itself, becoming a critical mass that is saying so in many different voices, languages, gestures, actions: *It must change; we ourselves can change it.*

We who are not the same. We who are many and do not want to be the same.

—Adrienne Rich, "Notes toward a Politics of Location"[1]

Identity would seem to be the garment with which one covers the nakedness of the self: in which case, it is best that the garment be loose, a little like the robes of the desert, through which robes one's nakedness can always be felt, and, sometimes, discerned. This trust in one's nakedness is all that gives one the power to change one's robes.

—James Baldwin, *The Devil Finds Work* (1976), text of Glenn Ligon's *Baldwin #4*, 1992

The impact on the visual arts of what is generally—if vaguely—termed the multiculturalist debate has been profound. Its effects are manifest discursively as well as institutionally, locally as well as internationally; they can be gauged by an increasing amount of critical writing and media coverage as well as by a growing number of exhibitions organized around multiculturalist themes (a selected list is provided on page 79). Even more significant has been the emergence of dozens of artists who have made questions of racial, ethnic, or sexual identity central themes in their work. *Mistaken Identities* and its catalog are thus meant to participate in a discourse that is as much political as cultural. Unlike earlier debates around postmodernism in the visual arts, multiculturalism cannot be detached from political actuality here and abroad, including the current cataclysms of ethnic and national strife, the ongoing struggles for empowerment by people of color, and the frightening upwellings of racism and xenophobia.

Where postmodernist art theory fostered a heightened awareness of the politics of representation, feminism and multiculturalism have quickened and mobilized those politics. This has been accomplished by anchoring relatively abstract analyses of power and ideology to their concrete and material effects, particularly as these act upon or are experienced by subaltern (that is to say, subordinated) subjects. Broadly speaking, postmodernist theory has examined the theoretical

Die auf Veränderung gerichtete Bewegung ist eine sich verändernde Bewegung; sie verändert sich selbst, entmännlicht sich selbst, entwestlicht sich selbst und wird so zu einer kritischen Masse, die in vielen verschiedenen Stimmen, Sprachen, Gesten, Handlungen sagt: Es muß sich ändern; wir selbst können es ändern.

Wir, die wir nicht die gleichen sind. Wir, die wir viele sind und nicht die gleichen sein wollen.

— Adrienne Rich, "Notes toward a Politics of Location"[1]

Identität ist wie das Gewand, mit dem man die Nacktheit des Ich bedeckt. Wenn es sich aber so verhält, dann ist es am besten, wenn das Gewand lose fällt, ein wenig wie der Burnus der Wüste, durch den die Nacktheit stets gefühlt und manchmal auch gesehen wird. Dieses Vertrauen auf die eigene Nacktheit ist es, die einem die Kraft gibt, die Kleider zu wechseln.

—James Baldwin, *Teufelswerk* (1976), Text von Glenn Ligons *Baldwin #4*, 1992

Die Auswirkungen dessen, was allgemein—wenn auch vage—als Multikulturalismus-Debatte bezeichnet wird, auf die bildende Kunst sind enorm. Sie zeigen sich auf der diskursiven Ebene ebenso wie auf der institutionellen, auf der lokalen ebenso wie auf der internationalen; sie sind ablesbar an der Zunahme der kritischen Schriften und der Medienberichterstattung sowie an der wachsenden Zahl der zu multikulturellen Themen organisierten Ausstellungen (eine Auswahl davon ist in diesem Katalog aufgelistet). Noch signifikanter aber ist das Auftauchen Dutzender Künstler, die Fragen rassischer, ethnischer oder sexueller Differenz zu zentralen Themen ihrer Arbeit gemacht haben. Die Ausstellung *Mistaken Identities* und ihr Katalog verstehen sich also als Beitrag zu einem Diskurs, der nicht minder politisch als kulturell ist. Denn anders als die frühere Postmodernismus-Diskussion ist der Multikulturalismus nicht zu trennen vom aktuellen politischen Geschehen im In- und Ausland, etwa den gegenwärtigen Ausbrüchen ethnischer und nationaler Zwistigkeiten, dem fortgesetzten Kampf farbiger Menschen um ihre Mitspracherechte und dem erschreckenden Wiederhochkommen von Rassismus und Fremdenhaß.

Hatte die postmoderne Kunsttheorie ein stärkeres Bewußtsein für die Politik der Repräsentation geschaffen, so haben Feminismus und Multikulturalismus diese Politik mobilisiert und zum Leben erweckt. Sie erreichten das, indem sie die relativ abstrakten Analysen von Macht und Ideologie an deren konkrete, materielle Auswirkungen knüpften, vornehmlich

construction of the Other in at least three overlapping forms: as an internal split in the subject, as the feminine Other of sexual difference, and as the Third World or diasporic Other—the "new" subject in history. However, it is feminism and multiculturalism that represent the lived subjectivity that postmodernism theorizes, the voices of those others. And while feminism and multiculturalism obviously have their academic incarnations, they are never *only* academic because they are also root and branch the expressions of political struggle. Within this struggle, culture—in both mass and elite forms—can be an important site for contestation and intervention.

Having said that, however, it is necessary immediately to add that multiculturalism in the arts—like the subject of identity itself—is by no means a self-evident or consensual concept. For example, is multiculturalism in the visual arts to be understood as a renewed version of cultural pluralism, a means by which the previously excluded gain entrance to the art-world emporium? Is it thus reducible to a politics of assimilation of what was previously euphemized as "minority" art? If this is so— if multiculturalism is taken to mean the assimilation of cultural difference to mainstream art culture— then it evades the more profound implications of its own critique. Which is to say that the significance of the multiculturalist debate does not so much lie in its recognition of diversity and difference per se, but in its consideration of differences, both in their historical specificity and in terms of the power relations in which they are moored.

The U.S. has always been a multicultural—and multiracial—society. Historically, this incontrovertible demographic fact has been framed within assimilationist models by which, for example, the singularity of the African-American or Native American experience has been incorporated (and simultaneously deracinated) within the model of European immigration. The pluralist acknowledgement of "diversity" has thus functioned to sidestep considerations of race and racism, to neutralize difference, just as it has blurred the distinctions between immigration, slavery, and the destruction of America's indigenous populations.

One legacy of the political and social movements and struggles born (or reborn) in the crucible of the '60s was to forever dispel the myth of the melting pot and its attendant fantasies of automatic assimilation. *E pluribus unum*, as it says on the dollar bill, has not only failed as hopeful prophecy, but been revealed as ideologically

deren Auswirkungen auf—und Erlebtwerden durch—subalterne (d.h. untergeordnete) Subjekte. Grob gesagt untersuchte die postmoderne Theorie die theoretische Konstruktion des Anderen in wenigstens drei einander überlappenden Formen: als innere Spaltung des Subjekts, als das weibliche Andere in der Geschlechtsdifferenz, als das Andere der Dritten Welt oder der Diaspora—das "neue" Subjekt in der Geschichte. Feminismus und Multikulturalismus aber *repräsentieren* die gelebte Subjektivität, die die Postmoderne theoretisch konstruiert hat: die Stimmen jener anderen. Und wenn zweifellos auch Feminismus und Multikulturalismus ihre akademischen Inkarnationen haben, so sind diese doch niemals *nur* akademisch, weil sie zugleich durch und durch Ausdruck eines politischen Kampfes sind. Im Rahmen dieses Kampfes kann Kultur—sowohl in ihrer populären als auch in ihrer elitären Form—ein wichtiger Schauplatz der Auseinandersetzung und Intervention sein.

Dies vorausgeschickt muß jedoch sofort hinzugefügt werden, daß der Multikulturalismus in der Kunst—ebenso wie die Frage der Identität selbst—keineswegs ein selbstverständlicher oder auch nur konsensualer Begriff ist. Ist Multikulturalismus in der bildenden Kunst etwa als Neuauflage eines kulturellen Pluralismus zu verstehen, als ein Weg, den ehemals Ausgeschlossenen Zutritt zu den Umschlagplätzen der Kunstwelt zu verschaffen? Ist er also reduzierbar auf eine Politik der Assimilation dessen, was man früher euphemistisch als "Minderheiten"-Kunst bezeichnete? Wenn dem so ist—wenn Multikulturalismus als Assimilation kultureller Differenz in die künstlerische Mainstream-Kultur aufgefaßt wird—, dann weicht er den tiefergehenden Implikationen seiner eigenen Kritik aus. Mit anderen Worten, die Signifikanz der Multikulturalismus-Debatte liegt weniger in der Anerkennung von Vielfalt und Differenz per se als vielmehr in der Betrachtung von Differenzen unter dem Gesichtspunkt sowohl ihrer spezifischen historischen Bedingtheit als auch der Machtverhältnisse, in denen sie verankert sind.

Die Vereinigten Staaten waren seit jeher eine multikulturelle—und multirassische—Gesellschaft. Traditionell wurde diese unbestreitbare demographische Tatsache mittels assimilatorischer Modelle erklärt, wodurch z.B. die Einzigartigkeit des Schicksals der Afroamerikaner oder der amerikanischen Ureinwohner dem europäischen Immigrationsmodell einverleibt (und damit ausgerottet) wurde. Das pluralistische Bekenntnis zur "Vielfalt" hat also dazu gedient, der Frage von Rasse und Rassismus auszuweichen, Differenz zu neutralisieren und die Unterschiede zwischen Immigration, Sklaverei und der Ausrottung der amerikanischen Urbevölkerung zu verwischen.

complicit in strategies of repression and erasure. Who or what is this "one" to be forged out of many? If, in our darkening fin-de-siècle, we see everywhere the conflicts and claims of difference, it must be acknowledged that all of our routinely-named distinctions—white/black, man/woman, straight/gay, plus all the hyphenated designations within nation and culture—are permeated with a violence that both underpins and ratifies their hierarchy. Insofar as it is always the second term that is "marked" as secondary, it necessarily follows that the mark of difference has been the inescapable burden of the Other.[2] From this recognition arises the politics of difference, be it a politics of affirmation ("Black is Beautiful," "Gay Pride") or a politics of opposition ("No justice, no peace").

What therefore distinguishes the multiculturalist paradigm in its contemporary formulations is its reevaluation of constitutive differences and the dominant culture's relation to them, and its raising of political and ethical questions about the role and consequences of these various differences within American (and by extension, European) life today.

Within this more politicized formulation, multiculturalism in the arts becomes not merely a question of who is doing the producing, but how that production relates to both art culture and culture at large. If multiculturalism in the arts is taken to mean a more activist, interventionist, and critical mobilization of the term "multiculturalism," it is then crucial to understand how "minority" or multicultural art production actually functions, and how it positions itself in relation to dominant modes of expression and ideology. In this case, it becomes important to retain the concepts and intentions of critical practice, encompassing its composite lineage in twentieth-century avant-gardes and Frankfurt School theorizations, as well as its most recent formulations within postmodernist cultural theory. This more politicized model of multiculturalism in the visual arts exceeds pluralism in both its political and aesthetic definitions, and it is this more politicized inflection of the term that has underpinned the organization of *Mistaken Identities*.

In contrast to the committed pluralism of such important exhibitions as the 1990 *The Decade Show*, or the 1991 *Interrogating Identity*, *Mistaken Identities* presents a range of art production in which the political aspects of multiculturalism are embodied in critical practices concerning the ways that identity—racial, ethnic, or

Ein Erbe der politischen und sozialen Bewegungen und Kämpfe, die aus der Feuerprobe der 60er Jahre hervorgingen (oder darin neu belebt wurden), besteht darin, daß sie den Mythos vom Schmelztiegel und die damit verbundenen Phantasien von automatischer Assimilation für immer zerstört haben. *E pluribus unum*, wie es auf der Dollarnote heißt, ist nicht nur als hoffnungsvolle Prophezeiung unerfüllt geblieben, sondern ist auch seiner ideologischen Komplizenschaft mit Unterdrückungs- und Auslöschungsstrategien überführt worden. Wer oder was ist dieses Eine, das aus den Vielen geschmiedet werden soll? Wenn wir in unserem sich verfinsternden Fin-de-siècle überall die Konflikte und Ansprüche der Differenz sehen, dann müssen wir erkennen, daß all unsere routiniert gebrauchten Unterscheidungen—weiß/schwarz, Mann/Frau, Hetero/Homo plus all die zusammengesetzten nationalen und kulturellen Etikettierungen—von einer Gewalt durchdrungen sind, die ihr hierarchisches Verhältnis sowohl belegt als auch ratifiziert. Insofern immer der zweite dieser Begriffe als sekundär "markiert" ist, ist das Mal der Differenz unweigerlich stets die Bürde des Anderen gewesen.[2] Dieser Erkenntnis entspringt die Politik der Differenz, sei es als eine Politik der Affirmation ("Black ist Beautiful", "Gay Pride") oder als eine Politik der Opposition ("No justice, no peace").

Was also das multikulturalistische Paradigma in seinen gegenwärtigen Ausformungen auszeichnet, ist seine Neubewertung konstitutiver Differenzen (wie auch des Verhältnisses der herrschenden Kultur diesen gegenüber) und das Aufwerfen politischer und ethischer Fragen hinsichtlich der Rolle und der Auswirkungen dieser diversen Differenzen innerhalb des heutigen Lebens in Amerika (und in weiterer Folge auch in Europa).

In dieser im strengeren Sinn politischen Ausprägung ist der Multikulturalismus in der Kunst nicht mehr bloß die Frage, wer die Produzenten sind, sondern in welchem Verhältnis ihre Produktion sowohl zur Kunst als auch zur Kultur im allgemeinen steht. Wenn Multikulturalismus in der Kunst eine aktivistischere, interventionistischere und kritischere Mobilisierung dieses Begriffs bedeuten soll, dann muß man verstehen, wie die multikulturelle Kunstproduktion—oder Kunstproduktion von "Minderheiten"—funktioniert und wie sie sich im Verhältnis zu den herrschenden Artikulationsweisen und Ideologien positioniert. Dafür ist es wichtig, die Konzepte und Intentionen einer kritischen Praxis beizubehalten, die sowohl die Traditionslinie umfaßt, die sich aus Avantgarde-Strömungen des 20. Jahrhunderts und Theorien der Frankfurter Schule zusammensetzt, als auch deren jüngste Ausformungen innerhalb der postmodernen Kulturtheorie. Dieses politisiertere

Fig. 2
Lorna Simpson
H.S., 1992
Cat. no. 19

Multikulturalismus-Modell in der bildenden Kunst geht über den Pluralismus—sowohl in seiner politischen als auch in seiner ästhetischen Dimension—hinaus und liegt—genau in diesem politischen Sinn—auch der Konzeption von *Mistaken Identities* zugrunde.

Im Gegensatz zum engagierten Pluralismus solch wichtiger Ausstellungen wie *The Decade Show* von 1990 oder *Interrogating Identity* von 1991 präsentiert *Mistaken Identities* ein Segment künstlerischer Produktion, in dem die politischen Aspekte des Multikulturalismus in kritischen Auseinandersetzungen mit der Art und Weise verkörpert sind, wie Identität—sei es die rassische, ethnische oder sexuelle—aufgezwungen, projiziert oder phantasiert wird. Solche Arbeiten erfüllen Baudelaires altehrwürdiges Diktum, "il faut être de son temps", in seinem strengsten Sinn, d.h. sie setzen sich mit den drängenden Problemen ihrer Zeit auseinander. Damit erfüllen sie eine der wichtigsten Funktionen von Kunst, eine Funktion, die man vielleicht als historisches Nachdenken über die Gegenwart in visueller Form beschreiben könnte.

Ob nun gefeiert oder beklagt—die Allgegenwärtigkeit und Unübersehbarkeit der Multikulturalismus-Diskussion ist mit den aktuellen Debatten über Identität eng verbunden. Umgekehrt sind auch die Identitätsdebatte und das Aufkommen der Identitätspolitik nicht von den Diskussionen rund um den Multikulturalismus zu trennen. Aber allein schon die Frage, *wie* Identität konstituiert wird, führt in den Bereich des Politischen hinein, denn sofern manche Identitäten mit Unterordnung und andere mit Herrschaft verbunden sind, besteht die Aufgabe ebensosehr in der Intervention wie in der Analyse.

Daß die Identitätsfrage so etwa in den letzten fünfzehn Jahren als zentrales Thema von Kunst in Erscheinung getreten ist, ist selbst eine stark überdeterminierte Entwicklung. Das Umfeld des Postkolonialismus, die Bildung neuer Nationen und Subjektivitäten, die durch den multinationalen Kapitalismus verursachten radikalen Entwurzelungen und Traumen, die wuchernden kulturellen Transformationen infolge der neuen Kommunikationstechnologien—das alles trägt auf einer globalen Bühne zur Umgestaltung und Neuformierung von kollektiven wie individuellen Identitäten bei. Keineswegs nur eine Abstraktion oder beschränkt auf den Bezirk des Persönlichen ist Identität heute mehr denn je ein Motor der Geschichte und ein Krisenauslöser. Diese ihre Januskopfigkeit—gleichermaßen Triebkraft für Emanzipation und Selbstbestimmung (in den nationalen Befreiungskämpfen in Indien, Afrika, Algerien, Indochina, in den sozialistischen Revolutionen in Kuba und Nicaragua) wie Saat für den todbringenden Sturm, der in den gegenwärtigen Bürgerkriegen

sexual—is imposed, projected, or fantasized. Such work fulfills Baudelaire's now hoary dictum, *"il faut être de son temps"* ("It is necessary to be of one's time") in its strongest sense; that is, it addresses itself to the urgent issues of the contemporary moment. In this, it performs one of the most serious functions of art, a function that might be described as thinking historically and in visual form about the present.

Whether celebrated or deplored, the ubiquity and prominence of the multicultural debate is closely tied to contemporary debates about identity. Conversely, debates about identity and the emergence of identity politics are inseparable from debates around multiculturalism. Furthermore, the very act of examining *how* identity is constituted opens onto the realm of the political, for insofar as certain identities entail subordination and others dominance, the task is one of intervention as well as analysis.

That the concept of identity *should* have emerged as a central theme for artists in the past fifteen years or so is itself a vastly overdetermined development. On a global stage, the frame of postcolonialism, the formation of new nations and subjectivities, the radical dislocations and traumas caused by multinational capitalism, the cultural transformations metastasized by new communication technologies all operate to refigure and refashion identities, both collective and individual. Far from being an abstraction or the limited province of the personal, identity is now more than ever a motor of history, a fulcrum of crisis. It is this Janus face—both a lever of emancipation and enfranchisement (as in the struggles for national liberation in India, Africa, Algeria, Indochina, the socialist revolutions in Cuba and Nicaragua) and a contributing factor in the lethal whirlwind reaped in ongoing civil wars—that makes any consideration of identity *as such* so difficult. If the internationalist ideals of nineteenth-century socialism, or of the secular and religious peace movements of the twentieth century seem currently moot, it is perhaps more than ever necessary to confront the issue head on.

Nonetheless, it is important to establish the specificity of the issues given form in *Mistaken Identities* and the contexts in which the art has been produced. For if indeed it is the case that the claims, contestations, and conundrums of individual and collective identity are everywhere manifest on the American scene, it by no means follows that "identity" in art or in life is either a

geerntet wird—macht auch jegliche Betrachtung von Identität *an sich* so schwer. Wenn das internationalistische Ideal des Sozialismus des neunzehnten Jahrhunderts oder der säkularen wie religiösen Friedensbewegungen des zwanzigsten heute fragwürdig erscheint, dann ist es vielleicht mehr denn je notwendig, das Problem frontal anzugehen.

Allerdings ist es wichtig, die Probleme, denen in *Mistaken Identities* Form verliehen wird, in ihrer jeweiligen Spezifizität herauszuarbeiten und festzustellen, in welchen Kontexten die Kunstwerke entstanden sind. Denn auch wenn die Ansprüche, Kontroversen und Kalamitäten individueller und kollektiver Identität tatsächlich überall auf der amerikanischen Szene zutage treten, so heißt das doch keineswegs, daß "Identität" in der Kunst oder im Leben ein einfacher oder unumstrittener Begriff ist. Wir sind in jedem Fall—an Jahren wie in unseren Überzeugungen—weit entfernt von den vermeintlichen Universalien und transzendenten Ansprüchen der modernistischen Malerei und Bildhauerei. Wir sind alle Bewohner einer Welt der Differenz, der Welt des postmodernen, postkolonialen, post-Kalter-Krieg-Subjekts. Die kritische Erkenntnis, daß dieses Subjekt durch Rasse, durch Klasse, durch Geschlecht gezeichnet und geformt ist, daß es geprägt ist durch eine Geschichte, die es entweder zu einem Nutznießer oder einem Opfer der bestehenden Weltordnung macht, ist der Anfang der Erkenntnis, daß die Einebnung von Differenz weder wünschenswert noch überhaupt möglich ist (Fig. 1 und 2). So betrachtet—und ungeachtet der Beschwörungen unseres gemeinsamen Menschseins—arbeiten die Künstler, die sich in ihrem Werk den Ansprüchen der Differenz verpflichtet fühlen, notgedrungen im Bereich des Politischen.

Die postmoderne Theorie selbst hat zum theoretischen Umfeld des Multikulturalismus und der Identitätsproblematik beigetragen, indem sie zum Beispiel mithalf, die Erforschung von Identität als zentralem Gegenstand künstlerischer Erkenntnis zu fördern. Die Konzentration der Postmoderne auf das Subjekt—seine Formation durch Kultur und Sprache und/oder seine historische Krise—hat ferner auch zu einer Beschäftigung mit den vielen Facetten der Identität und deren Zusammenwirken bei der Konstitution des Subjekts geführt. In dieser Hinsicht bleibt die Postmoderne ein unentbehrliches Modell für die begriffliche Erfassung eines tiefgreifenden Wandels der kulturellen Produktion in den letzten Jahrzehnten des Jahrhunderts. Im Hinblick auf die hier diskutierte Kunst könnte man diesen Wandel, vielleicht etwas verallgemeinernd, als die Abdankung des universellen Künstlers und die Geburt des spezifischen und historischen beschreiben.

simple or uncontested concept. We are in any case far—
in time and in belief—from the putative universals and
transcendent claims of modernist painting and sculpture.
We are all inhabitants of a world of difference, the world
of the postcolonial, post-Cold War, postmodern subject.
The critical recognition that this subject is marked and
shaped by race, by class, by gender, imprinted by histories
that make him or her a beneficiary or victim of the exist-
ing world order, is the beginning of a recognition that the
elision of difference is neither desirable nor, for that matter, possible (figs. 1 and 2). In this respect, and notwithstanding invocations of our common humanity, the artists
who construct their work in recognition of the claims of
difference are necessarily operating within the sphere of
the political.

Postmodern theory has itself contributed to the
theoretical formulations around multiculturalism and identity, serving, for example, to foster the exploration of identity as a prime object of artistic investigation. Furthermore,
postmodernism's focus on subjectivity—its formation in
culture and language and/or its historical crisis—has
evolved into a concern with the many facets of identity as
they collectively operate to constitute subjectivity. In this
respect, among others, postmodernism remains an indis-
pensable model for conceptualizing a profound shift in
cultural production in the closing decades of the century.
With respect to the art under discussion, this shift might be
described, somewhat sweepingly, as the demise of the universal artist and the birth of a specific and historical one.

Placing the art of *Mistaken Identities* under the
aegis of postmodernism is not, however, without its risks.
To the extent that postmodernist art was originally theorized with no reference whatsoever to artists of color, to
non-western cultural production, or to subaltern identities
(excepting, and that belatedly, women)[3] situating this art
in such a way can function as yet another form of cultural
imperialism. Consider, for example, Rasheed Araeen's
grim assessment:

> When the others begin to demand their share of the
> modern pie, modernism became post-modernism:
> now there is "Western" culture and "other" cultures
> located within the same "contemporary" space...the
> concept of "others" as mere victims of dominant
> culture will be to deny other cultures their ability to
> question their domination and to liberate themselves
> from it.[4]

Whether or not one agrees with Araeen's notion of postmodernist culture, his disenchantment with its terms is by

Die Kunstwerke von *Mistaken Identities* unter die
Ägide der Postmoderne zu stellen, ist jedoch nicht ohne Risi-
ken. Angesichts der Tatsache, daß farbige Künstler, nichtwest-
liche Kulturproduktion oder untergeordnete Identitäten (mit
der Ausnahme von Frauen und das mit Verspätung)[3] in der
urspünglichen Konzeption der postmodernen Kunst keinerlei
Berücksichtigung fanden, könnte sich eine solche Kontextuali-
sierung dieser Kunstwerke bloß als eine weitere Form von
Kulturimperialismus erweisen. Man denke nur an Rasheed
Araeens grimmiges Urteil:

> Als die anderen begannen, ihren Anteil am Kuchen der
> Moderne zu fordern, wurde die Moderne zur Postmo-
> derne: heute gibt es die "westliche" Kultur und "andere"
> Kulturen, situiert in ein- und demselben "zeitgenössi-
> schen" Raum... die Idee der "anderen" als bloßer Opfer
> der herrschenden Kultur wird dazu dienen, anderen
> Kulturen die Fähigkeit abzusprechen, ihre Beherrschung
> in Frage zu stellen und sich von ihr zu befreien.[4]

Ob man nun Araeens Sichtweise der postmodernen Kultur
teilt oder nicht, so sind doch farbige Künstler (und Kritiker)
nicht selten von den Begriffen der Postmoderne enttäuscht.
Auch viele andere scheinen nicht überzeugt von der diskursiven Überschreitung und/oder Subversion, die die postmoderne
Theorie für sich in Anspruch nimmt. So identifiziert sich etwa
Adrian Piper—in vieler Hinsicht *die* emblematische Künstlerin
dieser Ausstellung—nicht sonderlich mit dem Projekt des
Poststrukturalismus, das in der postmodernen Kulturtheorie
eine so zentrale Rolle spielte.[5]

Dennoch gibt es triftige Gründe, den begrifflichen
Rahmen der postmodernen Kunsttheorie als Grundschema für
die Ausstellung beizubehalten. Auf der augenscheinlichsten
Ebene sind da die künstlerischen Formen selbst—Foto/Text-
Arbeiten, Installation, Video/Installation—die man als quintes-
sentiell postmodern betrachten könnte. Unter den vielen
Künstlern in *Mistaken Identities* befindet sich nur ein einziger
Maler—Glenn Ligon—und selbst bei ihm sind die Gemälde
aus Texten komponiert, eine Form wörtlichen Zitierens.

Tiefergehend und entscheidender ist, daß die
Beschreibungs- und Definitionsversuche eines Konstrukts wie
"[British] Black Art"—zumindest nach der Meinung eines
Kommentators—praktisch ununterscheidbar sind von den
Begriffen, mit denen andere die postmoderne künstlerische
Praxis *tout court* beschrieben haben. So behauptet Sarat
Maharaj in seinem Essay, "The Congo is Flooding the Acropo-
lis: Black Art, Orders of Difference, Textiles", daß eines der
Unterscheidungsmerkmale der von ihm diskutierten Kunst
darin liege, daß sie die Codes der herrschenden Kultur gegen
diese ausspiele:

Fig. 3
Carrie Mae Weems
"Elaine," from *Four Women,* 1988
Cat. no. 24

no means infrequently encountered among artists (and critics) of color. Many others seem unpersuaded by postmodernist theory's claims to discursive transgression and/or subversion. Thus, Adrian Piper, who in many ways is *the* emblematic artist in this exhibition, does not especially identify herself with the poststructuralist project that has figured so prominently within postmodernist cultural theory.[5]

Nevertheless, there are valid reasons for retaining the terms of postmodernist art theory as an overall schema for the exhibition. On the most obvious level, the artistic forms themselves—photo/text works, installation, video/installation—may be considered as quintessentially postmodern. Of the many artists in *Mistaken Identities,* only one—Glenn Ligon—is a painter, but even here, the paintings are composed of texts, a form of literal quoting.

More suggestively, attempts to describe and define what at least one commentator wants to theorize as [British] "Black Art" are virtually indistinguishable from the terms others have used to designate postmodern art practices *tout court*. Thus, in his essay "The Congo is Flooding the Acropolis: Black Art, Orders of Difference, Textiles," Sarat Maharaj argues that one of the distinguishing features of the art he discusses resides in its playing off the codes of the dominant culture:

Der Antrieb hinter dem oppositionellen Gestus [der "Black Art"] scheint der Wunsch zu sein, einen Standpunkt außerhalb des herrschenden Repräsentationssystems zu finden, von dem aus man es anklagen und geißeln kann, von dem aus man seine Art, sich und andere darzustellen, transformieren und umwälzen kann. Ein solcher Außenstandpunkt ist allerdings weniger, wie es scheint, irgendwo "dort draußen" fix und fertig vorzufinden, sondern muß vielmehr mühsam von innen heraus konstruiert werden. Er muß paradoxerweise aus dem, was "innen" ist, gebildet werden, aus den Elementen genau jenes Repräsentationssystems, über das er hinaus will... Es ist, als entwickle die "Black Art" ihre Kritik aus einer ursprünglichen Komplizenschaft mit dem von ihr kritisierten Material, als forme sie ihr Gefühl der kritischen Distanz, indem sie sich zuerst mit dem vereinigt, was sie sich vom Leib halten will.[6]

Maharajs Charakterisierung dessen, was er "Black Art" nennt, ist eigentlich eine Formulierung postmoderner Zitatstrategien, die sich auf Massenmedien oder andere dominante Repräsentationssysteme beziehen. Die Berufung auf diese Taktik zur begrifflichen Abgrenzung einer eigenen "Black Art" mutet merkwürdig an—vor allem deshalb, weil die erörterten Künstler—wie auch die farbigen Künstler dieser Ausstellung—nicht entscheidend anders zu arbeiten scheinen (von Thema und Gegenstand einmal abgesehen) als ihre Kollegen. Im Gegenteil: wenn farbige Künstler auf irgendeine legitime Weise *separat* von anderen Künstlern im kulturellen Umfeld der Postmoderne diskutiert werden können, dann

The drive behind [Black Art's] oppositional mode seems to be the desire to find some stance outside the prevailing system of representation from which to impeach and castigate it, from which to overturn and transform its way of picturing self and other. But such an outside standpoint, it would appear, is not so much found ready-made "out there" as it has to be painfully constructed from within. It has to be forged, quite paradoxically, from the "inside" out of elements of the very system of representation it seeks to go beyond.... It is as if Black Art creates its critique through an initial complicity with the material it denounces, carves out its sense of critical distance by first becoming one with what it intends to keep at arm's length.[6]

Maharaj's characterization of what he terms Black Art is in fact a restatement of postmodernism's quotational strategies, derived either from mass media or other dominant representational systems. That these tactics should be invoked in the service of conceptualizing a distinctive "Black Art" seems curious, particularly in that the artists he discusses, like the artists of color in this exhibition, do not appear to be working in ways (themes and subject matter notwithstanding) markedly different from those of their peers. On the contrary, if artists of color can legitimately be discussed *apart* from other artists situated within the cultural space of postmodernism, it is with respect to their willingness to address problems of identity and subjectivity while acknowledging the limits and possibilities of postmodernism's analysis of material and institutional power.

But in characterizing the art of *Mistaken Identities* under the sign of postmodernism, I am thinking less of the now-familiar tropes and strategies of postmodernist artmaking (e.g., appropriation, pastiche, engagement with mass cultural forms—although these can certainly be found in much of this work) than I am of postmodernism's concern with the politics of representation. Clearly the issue of representational politics has particular urgency in the case of those who have historically been denied the means of self-representation, encapsulated in Marx's description of the colonized "who do not represent themselves, [but] are represented."

In this sense, Carrie Mae Weems' photographic reiteration of the most obscene and degrading stereotypes of black men and women, as in her *Jokes* series or, for that matter, in her *Black Man with Watermelon* and *Black Woman with Chicken* (fig. 4), are especially interesting. Such works are uncompromisingly confrontational and deeply uncomfortable, as provocative and unpalatable to

wegen ihrer Bereitschaft, sich mit Problemen der Identität und Subjektivität unter Anerkennung der Grenzen und Möglichkeiten der postmodernen Analyse materieller und institutioneller Macht auseinanderzusetzen.

Wenn ich die Kunstwerke in *Mistaken Identities* unter einem postmodernen Gesichtspunkt charakterisiere, denke ich allerdings weniger an die heute geläufigen Tropen und Strategien postmoderner künstlerischer Verfahrensweisen (wie Zitat, Pastiche, das Arbeiten mit Formen der Massenkultur—obwohl auch das natürlich in vielen dieser Werke zu finden ist), sondern ich denke eher an das Interesse der Postmoderne für die Politik der Repräsentation. Die besondere Dringlichkeit der Frage der Repräsentationspolitik im Falle derer, denen die Mittel der Selbstrepräsentation historisch vorenthalten wurden, derer, die sich nach Marx' Beschreibung der Kolonisierten "nicht selbst vertreten, [sondern] vertreten werden", liegt auf der Hand.

Besonders interessant in dieser Hinsicht sind Carrie Mae Weems' fotografische Wiederholungen der obzönsten und übelsten schwarzen Männer- und Frauenstereotypen wie in ihrer Serie *Jokes* oder in *Black Man with Watermelon* und *Black Woman with Chicken* (Fig. 4). Diese Arbeiten sind kompromißlose und zutiefst beunruhigende Attacken, die für manche weißen Betrachter nicht weniger provokativ und ungenießbar sind als für schwarze.[7] Was nicht heißen soll, daß der Skandal—etwa von *What are three things you can't give a black person*—bei schwarzen Betrachtern auf dieselbe Weise wirkt wie bei nichtschwarzen. Mit der—wenn auch bewußt ästhetisierten—Reproduktion rassistischer Stereotypen macht Weems etwas ähnliches wie (in ihren früheren Arbeiten) Cindy Sherman, die sich ebenfalls als Hoflieferantin von Stereotypen—in ihrem Fall einem Lexikon der Weiblichkeit—betätigte. In Weems' *Four Women* (Fig. 3) liegt die Analogie sogar noch näher, da sie sich darin selbst etwa in der Rolle einer militanten Schwarzen, einer afrikanischen Nationalistin oder einer bürgerlichen Hausfrau in Szene setzt. Aber der Akt der Wiederholung, der Re-präsentation des rassistischen Stereotyps, hat auch mit Mimikry zu tun, einer Strategie, die ebenfalls als eine Form subalternen Widerstands gedeutet wurde.[8] Tatsächlich sind die Aneignung von Stereotypen und die strategische Verwendung von Mimikry als typische Formen afroamerikanischer "Signifikation" charakterisiert worden—eine hybride Form des kulturellen Widerstands und Überlebenskampfes.[9] Diese Verwendung des bereits Bekannten, bereits Gesehenen (egal wie geschmacklos oder fromm verleugnet) ist aber auch ein Merkmal postmoderner Praktiken. Auch wenn

BLACK WOMAN WITH CHICKEN

Fig. 4
Carrie Mae Weems
Black Woman with Chicken
1987
Cat. no. 23

certain white viewers as to black.[7] Which is not to say that the scandal of, for example, *What are three things you can't give to a black person?* functions in the same way for black and non-black viewers. In reproducing the racist stereotype, albeit in deliberately aestheticized form, Weems is doing something akin to the earlier work of Cindy Sherman, who likewise trafficked in the purveyal of stereotypes—in Sherman's case, a lexicon of femininity. In Weems' *Four Women* (fig. 3), the analogy is even closer, as Weems herself stages the roles of, for example, black militant, African nationalist, and bourgeois housewife. But the act of reiteration, the re-presentation of the racist stereotype, partakes as well in the strategy of mimicry, a strategy that has been theorized as itself a form of subaltern resistance.[8] The appropriation of the stereotype and the strategic use of mimicry have in fact been characterized as distinctive modes of African-American "signifying"—a hybrid mode of cultural resistance and survival.[9] This deployment of the already-known, already-seen (no matter how distasteful or piously disavowed) is also a hallmark of postmodernist practice. And while Weems brings to her work the knowledge and perceptions of a trained folklorist, the programmatic and artful repetition of the racist stereotype is equally a quotational device consistent with the tropes of postmodernism. It is significant too that Weems—like all the artists in this exhibition—rejects the notion of what might be called representational reparations, that is, the countering of degrading and racist imagery with "real" or "true" or "positive" depictions of black people. Although it would

Fig. 5
Marlon Riggs
video still from *Tongues Untied*, 1989
Cat. no. 29

Weems in ihre Arbeit das Wissen und die Beobachtungen der ausgebildeten Volkskundlerin einbringt, so ist die programmatische und kunstvolle Wiederholung des rassistischen Stereotyps doch zugleich auch ein Zitatverfahren, das sich mit den Tropen der Postmoderne deckt. Bezeichnend ist auch, daß Weems—wie alle anderen Künstler dieser Ausstellung—ablehnt, was man vielleicht als Wiedergutmachungsrepräsentation bezeichnen könnte, also die Kompensation erniedrigender und rassistischer Bilder durch "wirkliche" oder "wahre" oder "positive" Darstellungen von Schwarzen. Man könnte zwar behaupten, daß das traumhaft schöne Modell in "Woman with Chicken" und die emotionale Kraft ihres Blicks ein solches Korrektiv darstellt, zumeist aber arbeitet Weems kompromißlos im Bereich des Stereotyps. Und auch dieser kritische Einsatz des Stereotyps zur Sichtbarmachung seiner bösartigen Wirkungen ist wiederum ein fixer Bestandteil postmoderner Kunst, der zumindest bis zur Arbeit von Sherrie Levine und Richard Prince zurückreicht.

Während Weems Identität im blinden Spiegel des Stereotyps einfaßt, geht Marlon Riggs' *Tongues Untied* Identität (in seinem Fall die des schwarzen Homosexuellen) von der anderen Seite her an, d.h. in einem affirmativen und *kollektiven* Akt der Selbstbenennung (Fig. 5). *Tongues Untied* demonstriert die politische Strategie der Affirmation einer sozial dämonisierten Identität mit emanzipatorischen Zielen. So setzt der wiederkehrende Slogan—"Black men loving black men is *the* revolutionary act"—eine sexuelle Vorliebe mit politischem Kampf gleich. Indem er die Identität des "schwulen Schwarzen" als gegeben voraussetzt und deren erotische und diskursive Ausdrucksformen zelebriert, geht es Riggs' Film weniger um die Konstruktion dieser Identität als um deren provozierende Überschreitung dominanter (und repressiver) Bilder von Männlichkeit, egal ob schwarz oder weiß. In dieser Hinsicht unterscheidet sich *Tongues Untied* von den meisten Arbeiten dieser Ausstellung. Insofern der Film aber eine künstlerische Selbstermächtigungsstrategie durch Selbstbenennung und andere Mittel demonstriert, erinnert er uns daran, daß die kollektive Identitätspolitik (im Film beispielsweise repräsentiert durch die Darstellung von Straßenaktionen und Demonstrationen) ein machtvoller Motor des politischen Kampfes ist. Wenn man also sagen könnte, daß Weems Identität und Subjektivität unter dem Aspekt ihres Unterworfenseins betrachtet, dann zelebriert Riggs deren aktive Manifestationen. Diese beiden Aspekte von Identität—das Subjekt als Unterworfenes und das Subjekt als aktiv Handelndes—markieren die Grenzen und Möglichkeiten der Subjektivität; und die Spannung zwischen ihnen, die in dieser Ausstellung

be possible to claim that the haunting beauty of the model in *Black Woman with Chicken* and the emotional power of her gaze constitutes such a corrective, for the most part Weems operates uncompromisingly in the realm of the stereotype. Here again, the deployment of the stereotype in ways that render its malignant operations critically visible has been a staple of postmodernist art, going back at least to Sherrie Levine's and Richard Prince's work of the late 1970s.

Where Weems brackets identity behind the glass darkly of the stereotype, Marlon Riggs' *Tongues Untied* approaches identity (in this instance, black, gay male identity) from the opposite direction, that is to say, within an affirmative and *collective* act of self-naming (fig. 5). *Tongues Untied* demonstrates the political strategy of affirming a socially demonized identity for emancipatory ends. The recurring banner—"Black men loving black men is *the* revolutionary act"— thus equates sexual preference with political struggle. In taking the identity "gay black male" as a given, and celebrating its erotic and discursive expression, Riggs' film is concerned less with the construction of that identity than with its defiant transgression of dominant (and oppressive) notions of masculinity, black or white. In this respect, *Tongues Untied* differs somewhat from most of the work in this exhibition. But insofar as it demonstrates an artistic strategy of empowerment through self-naming as well as other means, it reminds us that collective identity politics (represented, for example, in the film's depiction of street politics and demonstrations) is a powerful motor of political struggle. Thus, where Weems can be said to consider subjectivity and identity from the perspective of subjection, Riggs celebrates the manifestations of agency. These twin facets of identity—the subject as subjected and the subject as agent—mark the limits and possibilities of subjectivity, and it is the tension between the two, evident in much of this exhibition, that complicates a too facile opposition between "identity politics" and social constructivism.

What primarily separates the works of artists like Weems and Riggs from those generally grouped in the category of critical or oppositional postmodernism is their recognition of the *specificity* of issues of identity and subjectivity as they are experienced by people of color and other subaltern groups. This, too, is shaped by multiculturalist and postmodernist theories, both of which have prompted artists to reclaim subjectivity as an object

sehr oft zu spüren ist, kompliziert auch eine zu einfache Opposition zwischen "Identitätspolitik" und sozialem Konstruktivismus.

Was die Arbeiten von Künstlern wie Weems und Riggs von denen, die gewöhnlich unter der Rubrik kritischer oder oppositioneller Postmodernismus zusammengefaßt werden, zunächst unterscheidet, ist ihre Berücksichtigung der *Spezifizität* der von Farbigen und anderen Minderheiten erlebten Identitäts- und Subjektivitätsproblematik. Auch dies ist durch multikulturelle und postmoderne Theorien vorgeprägt, die die Künstler dazu angeregt haben, sich Subjektivität als ästhetischen Erkenntnisgegenstand zurückzuerobern. Diese Subjektivität hat jedoch wenig Ähnlichkeit mit ihrem modernen Vorläufer, denn sie wird als historisch-politische und als psychologische gesehen. Nicht der universelle und transzendentale Künstler spricht hier, sondern der einzelne und historische. Dieses Beharren auf dem Spezifischen erlaubt es diesen Künstlern auch, metaphorische Formulierungen—wie die von der Unsichtbarkeit der farbigen Frau—in konkreten Verkörperungen greifbar zu machen.

Bei der Konzeption von *Mistaken Identities* unter Berücksichtigung der Komplexität und Verschiedenartigkeit der Argumentionsweisen in Bezug auf Identität und Multikulturalismus—sei es theoretisch, politisch oder praktisch—ging es weniger darum, eine kohärente, repräsentable Position zu entwickeln, als darum, Arbeiten zusammenzutragen, die sich auf unterschiedliche Weise mit der Problematik der Identität auseinandersetzen. Wir waren interessiert an künstlerischen Praktiken, die entweder bemüht sind, die psychischen und/oder sozialen Komponenten zu zeigen, aufgrund deren verschiedene Identitäten von außen zugeschrieben oder phantasmatisch projiziert werden (Williams, Rosler, Kelly, Hatch, Tabrizian und Golding, Weems), die eine vorläufige, bricolageartige Formation von Identität nahelegen (Durham, Gómez-Peña, Hak Kyung Cha, Rascón, Yong Soon Min) oder die die vermeintlichen Unveränderlichkeiten von Rasse und rassischem Denken destabilisieren und dekonstruieren (Ligon, Piper).

Die in dieser Ausstellung gemeinsam erforschten Identitäten sind also "mißverstandene" insofern, als sie niemals als *ein Ding* gedacht wurden, ob dieses Ding nun Rasse, Geschlecht oder ethnische Zugehörigkeit heißt. Die Palette der Künstler und die Vielfalt der Praktiken zeigen, daß das vielgestaltige und wechselnde Feld der Identität—in seiner subjektiven und erlebten Realität—eingebettet ist in Geschichte, in Diskurs, in Kontext und daß es daher niemals eine einfache, unproblematische Gegebenheit ist. Die Zusammenstellung einer Gruppe von Künstlern, deren gemeinsamer

for aesthetic exploration. This subjectivity, however, resembles little its modernist ancestor, because the subjectivity investigated is apprehended historically and politically as well as psychologically. It is not the generic, transcendental Artist who speaks, but the singular, historical one. Similarly, this insistence on specificity enables these artists to grasp metaphorical formulations—for example, the invisibility of the woman of color—and give them concrete embodiment.

However, in organizing *Mistaken Identities* with cognizance of the complexity and diversity of the arguments—theoretical, political and practical—around identity and multiculturalism, the idea was less to produce a coherent and unified position than to assemble works that are variously engaged with what could be termed the problematics of identity. We were interested in art practices that are either concerned to demonstrate the psychic and/or social components by which diverse identities are attributed or fantasmatically projected (cf., Williams, Rosler, Kelly, Hatch, Tabrizian and Golding, Weems); that suggested the provisional, bricolage-like formation of identity (cf., Durham, Gómez-Peña, Hak Kyung Cha, Rascón, Yong Soon Min); or those that dismantled or deconstructed the putative fixities of race and racialism (cf., Ligon, Piper).

The identities collectively explored in this exhibition are thus "mistaken" insofar as they have ever been imagined or conceived as *one thing*, whether that thing was identified as race, gender, or ethnicity. This range of artists and diversity of practices demonstrate that the multiple and shifting field of identity in its subjective and experiential reality is embedded in history, in discourse, in context, and is thus never a simple and unproblematic given. Assembling a group of artists whose common denominator is the rejection of what I have termed representational reparation (unless one considers the imaging of what has been overwhelmingly obscured as itself a form of reparation), the intention is to shift the burden of reparation from the artist to the curator, the critic, the institution. In this respect, the marginalization of the art world's "others" has been no less a consequence of the myopia of critics, myself included, who while defining themselves as feminists, and proponents of an oppositional postmodernism, were nonetheless blind to the claims of those very differences our critical apparatus ritualistically invoked. This systematic, if unwitting practice of omission and exclusion demonstrates as clearly as

Nenner in ihrer Ablehnung dessen besteht, was ich Wiedergutmachungsrepräsentation genannt habe (will man nicht schon in der Darstellung dessen, was so massiv unsichtbar gemacht wurde, eine Wiedergutmachung sehen), verfolgt die Absicht, die Last der Wiedergutmachung vom Künstler auf den Kurator, den Kritiker, die Institution zu verlagern. Denn die Marginalisierung der "anderen" in der Kunstwelt war auch eine Folge der Kurzsichtigkeit der Kritiker (ich eingeschlossen), die wir uns selbst als Feministinnen und Proponenten einer oppositionellen Postmoderne definierten und doch taub waren gegenüber den Ansprüchen derer, deren Differenzen unser kritischer Apparat rituell zu beschwören pflegte. Diese ungewollte, aber systematische Auslassungs- und Ausgrenzungspraxis zeigt deutlich genug, wer die Last der Wiedergutmachung zu tragen hat. Dazu kommt, daß uns jede Konfrontation mit den Fragen, die durch Multikulturalismus und Identität in der bildenen Kunst aufgeworfen werden, deutlich werden läßt, daß das "Politische" keineswegs ein klar umgrenzter Bezirk jener Künstler ist, die es offen als Grundlage ihrer Arbeit deklarieren, sondern—noch fundamentaler sogar—die unausweichliche Bedingung unserer Aktivitäten in den institutionellen und diskursiven Räumen der Kultur.

Auf diesem theoretischen Fundament richtete sich die Gestaltung der Ausstellung an einer Politik der Form aus. Das Fehlen traditioneller Medien, gegenständlicher Malerei oder "realistischer" Ausdrucksformen ist also durchaus Absicht.[10] Außerdem werden in fast allen gezeigten Arbeiten Texte verwendet. Das bringt bei einer nicht für den englischsprachigen Raum bestimmten Ausstellung zwar Probleme mit sich, aber die allgegenwärtige Verwendung von Texten und Zitaten ist nicht nur ein Erbe der Konzeptkunst, sondern auch ein Merkmal für das den Künstlern gemeinsame Bewußtsein, daß Rasse, Geschlecht und ethnische Zugehörigkeit Entitäten sind, die in und mit Sprache produziert und reproduziert werden.

Die Künstler in *Mistaken Identities* unterstreichen wie die Konzeptualisten, daß Kunst auf zahlreichen Ebenen außerhalb des "rein Visuellen" statthat, daß ihr Sinn und ihre Wirkung immer schon eingebettet ist in diese "andere Szene" der Repräsentation und daß schließlich die Probleme der Subjektivität (der des Künstlers wie der des Betrachters) untrennbar verbunden sind mit den sprachlichen Strukturen, die sie formen.

Das Element der Sprache in so vielen Arbeiten von *Mistaken Identities*—vor allem in den Arbeiten von farbigen Künstlern—hat aber eine ganz spezifische Funktion. Sie zeigt, wie der Sprachgebrauch (und dazu gehört auch der Akt des Benennens) das Material und die institutionellen Strukturen

Dear Friend,
I am black.
I am sure you did not realize this when you made/laughed at/agreed with that racist remark. In the past, I have attempted to alert white people to my racial identity in advance. Unfortunately, this invariably causes them to react to me as pushy, manipulative, or socially inappropriate. Therefore, my policy is to assume that white people do not make these remarks, even when they believe there are no black people present, and to distribute this card when they do.
I regret any discomfort my presence is causing you, just as I am sure you regret the discomfort your racism is causing me.

Fig. 6
Adrian Piper
My Calling (Card) #1, 1986
Cat. no. 12

anything where the burden of reparation must fall. Furthermore, any engagement with the issues raised around multiculturalism and identity in the visual arts reminds us that the "political" is by no means a circumscribed property of those artists who would openly claim it as a foundation of their artmaking, but even more fundamentally, is an inescapable condition of our activities in the institutional and discursive spaces of culture.

With this as the theoretical underpinning, the shaping of the exhibition was predicated on a politics of form. The absence of traditional media, figurative painting, or "realist" modes of expression is thus quite deliberate.[10] Furthermore, almost every work in the exhibition features the use of text. While this presents real problems in an exhibition destined for non-Anglophone venues, the ubiquity of textual use or citation is not only a legacy of conceptualism, but a feature of the artists' collective awareness that race, gender, and ethnicity are entities produced and reproduced within language.

As with conceptualism, the artists in *Mistaken Identities* confirm that art functions on many levels beyond the "purely visual," that its meanings and address are always and already implicated in this "other scene" of representation, and lastly, that issues of subjectivity (the artist's or the viewer's) are inseparable from the linguistic structures that forge this subjectivity.

But the agency of language in so much of the work in *Mistaken Identities*—particularly that produced by artists of color—has a quite specific aspect, signaling the ways in which linguistic use (including the act of naming) produces and reproduces the material and the institutional structures of racism, xenophobia, class, and gender that are part of the perception of difference. To take two highly contrasting examples, consider the deadpan *politesse* of the text used in Adrian Piper's *My Calling (Card) #1* (fig. 6). In a precise and pointed way, it informs the recipient that they have made a racist remark in the mistaken belief that their interlocutor was white. It could

von Rassismus, Fremdenangst, Klasse und Geschlecht produziert und reproduziert, die ein Teil der Wahrnehmung von Differenz sind. Zwei sehr gegensätzliche Beispiele sollen das demonstrieren. Betrachten wir einmal die distanzierte Politesse des Textes von Adrian Pipers *My Calling (Card) #1* (Fig. 6). Auf präzise und pointierte Weise läßt er den Empfänger wissen, daß dieser in der falschen Annahme, sein Gesprächspartner sei weiß, eine rassistische Bemerkung gemacht hat. Obwohl man die Arbeit selbst als eine Spracharbeit bezeichnen könnte, ist sie wohl treffender als eine soziale Interaktionsarbeit zu beschreiben, da ihre Bedeutung letztlich in ihrer Wirkung auf den Empfänger liegt. Dennoch ist das, was dieses Kunstwerk trägt, die Sprache, Sprache in ihrer unästhetischsten, geradlinigsten Form. Der Titel, dessen Witz darin liegt, daß er gezielten Anti-Rassismus als eine Art Beruf(ung) ausweist, evoziert gleichzeitig auch eine andere, ältere Bedeutung der Visitenkarte. Als Ausdruck einer (bürgerlichen) Identität, die so persönlich ist wie ein Name und so sozial wie eine Klasse, tut die traditionelle Visitenkarte—nicht zu verwechseln mit der modernen Geschäftskarte—die Existenz, soziale Sichtbarkeit und weltliche Position ihres Besitzers kund. Orlando Pattersons Charakterisierung des Sklaven-Status als eine Art "sozialen Todes" zeigt, wie scharfsinnig Pipers Reaktion ist.[11] Indem sie gegen Rassismus im Zeichen vornehmer Höflichkeit auftritt, ist die Form der Visitenkarte zurückhaltend und explosiv zugleich. In diesem Sinn hat Piper selbst eloquent zur moralischen Logik der Etikette geschrieben:

> Die Normen der Etikette regeln den Umgang der Individuen miteinander. Anders als andere Normen funktionieren (oder versagen) sie unabhängig von der Klasse oder vom ökonomischen Status. Zur Etikette der Anerkennung von kulturell und ethnisch anderen gehören Normen der Höflichkeit (die rassistische oder sexistische Fehltritte ausschließen), der "noblesse oblige" (die die selbstverliebte Verachtung oder Gleichgültigkeit gegenüber weniger Glücklichen ausschließen), der Demut und Bescheidenheit (was die Frage betrifft, wer denn überhaupt der weniger Glückliche ist und in welcher Hinsicht), des Taktes (Normen, die Sensibilität für die Gefühle anderer fordern unabhängig von ihrer kulturellen oder ethnischen Zugehörigkeit) und ein Sinn für

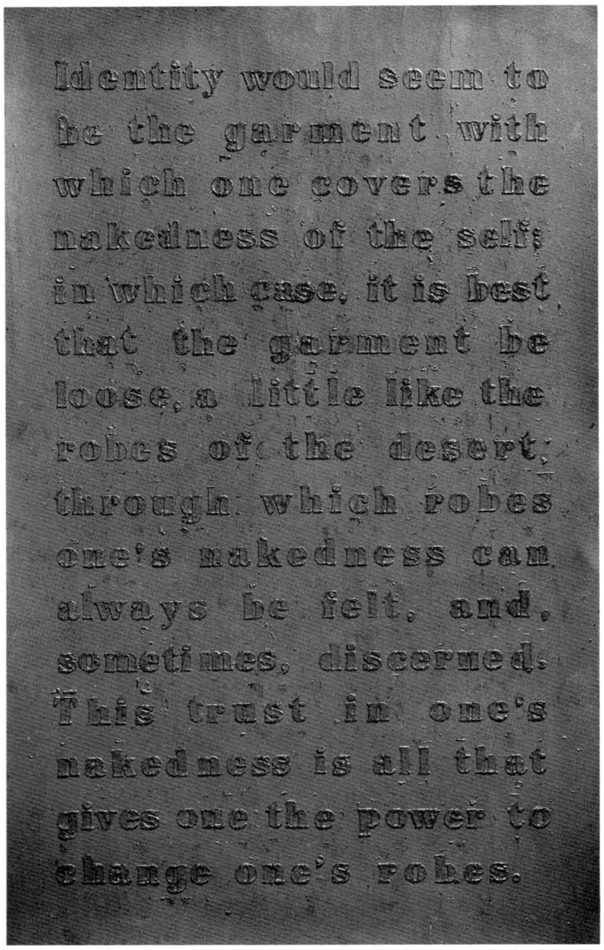

Fig. 7
Glenn Ligon
Baldwin #4 (Identity Would
Seem...), 1992
Cat. no. 10

be said that the "work" is itself a work of language, but it is more accurately described as a work of social interaction, since its import is ultimately located in its effect on the recipient. Nonetheless, it is language that carries the art, and language in its most de-aestheticized, plainspoken form. The wit of the title, which identifies purposeful anti-racism as a type of vocation, evokes as well another, older meaning of a calling card. A statement of (bourgeois) identity that is as personal as a name but as broadly social as a class, the traditional calling card—not to be confused with the modern business card—announces the bearer's existence, social visibility, and worldly position. Orlando Patterson's characterization of slave status as "social death" suggests the profundity of Piper's response.[11] Countering racism with a token of gentility, the calling card format is simultaneously both demure and explosive. In this respect, Piper has written eloquently on the moral logic of etiquette:

Würde (wozu gehört, daß man andere genauso respektvoll behandelt, wie man selbst behandelt werden möchte). Gemessen an diesen Normen sind Rassismus und Sexismus nicht nur ungerecht und unmoralisch, sondern auch ungehobelt und geschmacklos, und wer diese, wo immer, offen praktiziert, erweist sich als vulgär und schlecht erzogen.[12]

Im Gegensatz zum instrumentellen und direkten Sprachgebrauch Pipers ist die Sprache in Ligons Arbeiten durchweg literarisch. Die Zitate (zu den Schriftstellern, die er verwendet hat, gehören James Baldwin, Zora Neale Hurston, Mary Wollstonecraft und Jean Genet) sprechen vielfach von Rasse und Identität. Das Textzitat ist aber in den meisten von Lignons Arbeiten zugleich der *Stoff* der Malerei selbst; die Schrift wird ebenso als malerisches Zeichen verwendet wie als Transportmittel von Inhalten. Auf ganz ähnliche Weise wie sich in Mary Kellys *Interim* (als Ganzes) eine komplexe und kritische Beziehung zu ihren konzeptuellen und minimalistischen Vorläufern manifestiert, führen Ligons Textgemälde

Norms of etiquette govern interpersonal treatment of individuals. Unlike many other kinds of norms, they function (or fail to function) independently of class and economic status. Norms of etiquette that express acceptance of cultural and ethnic others include norms of courtesy (which exclude racist or sexist slurs), of noblesse oblige (which exclude self-serving contempt for or indifference to the less fortunate), of modesty and humility (about who is in fact less fortunate than whom, and in what respects), of tact (which presuppose sensitivity to others' feelings irrespective of cultural or ethnic affiliation), and a sense of honor (which includes extending to others the same respectful treatment one expects for oneself). Judged against these norms, racism and sexism are not only unjust and immoral. They are also boorish and tasteless; and those who practice them overtly in any context betray vulgarity and inferior breeding.[12]

Unlike Piper's instrumental and direct address, language in Ligon's work is consistently literary. The citations (the writers he has used include James Baldwin, Zora Neale Hurston, Mary Wollstonecraft, and Jean Gênet) speak variously of race and identity. But in most of Ligon's works the textual citation is the very *stuff* of the paintings; writing is used as painterly sign as well as the vehicle of content. In much the way that Mary Kelly's *Interim* (in its entirety) manifests a complex and critical relationship to her conceptual and minimalist predecessors, Ligon's text paintings enact a critical dialogue with late modernist abstraction. Nowhere is this relationship clearer than in *Baldwin #4* (fig. 7), an acrylic on paper work which, when covered with Plexiglas, appears on first sight to be an undifferentiated black ground or, as one approaches, a subtle variation of black-on-black, evoking, for example, the famous black paintings of Ad Reinhardt. In fact, like Ligon's previous work, *Baldwin #4* is equally a painting *of* a text and a text as painting, or a painting *as* text.

At least implicitly, *Baldwin #4* offers a critical commentary on the pretensions of '50s abstraction. For despite their strenuous aspirations to sublimity, universalism, and transcendence, the paintings of artists such as Barnett Newman and Ad Reinhardt have been historically revealed to be as contingent and contextually bound as any other "period" style. In this respect, Ligon conscripts what seems like a paradigmatic high-modernist form—a black on black painting—to radically different ends. For example, the Plexiglas covering, which obscures the text, is also a reflective surface; as the viewer deciphers the text, the work insistently mirrors her own reflection. Modernism's concern with self-reflexivity is here given a particular spin, turned—*détourné*—back upon the

einen kritischen Dialog mit der spätmodernistischen Abstraktion. Nirgendwo ist diese Beziehung deutlicher als in *Baldwin # 4* (Fig. 7), einer Acrylarbeit auf Papier, die—hinter Plexiglas—auf den ersten Blick wie eine undifferenzierte schwarze Fläche wirkt oder—beim Näherkommen—wie eine zarte Schwarz-auf-Schwarz-Variation—etwa von der Art der berühmten schwarzen Bilder von Ad Reinhardt. Tatsächlich ist *Baldwin # 4*—wie Ligons frühere Arbeiten—gleichermaßen das Gemälde *von* einem Text wie ein Gemälde *als* Text oder ein Text als Gemälde.

Zumindest implizit liefert *Baldwin # 4* einen kritischen Kommentar zu den Prätentionen der abstrakten Malerei der 50er Jahre. Denn trotz ihrer angestrengten Bemühungen um Erhabenheit, Universalismus und Transzendenz sind die Gemälde von Künstlern wie Barnett Newman und Ad Reinhardt, wie die Geschichte gezeigt hat, genauso zeitbedingt und kontextgebunden wie jeder andere "Epochenstil". Insofern zieht Ligon eine scheinbar paradigmatische hochmodernistische Form—ein Schwarz-auf-Schwarz-Gemälde—für radikal andere Zwecke heran. Die Plexi-Abdeckung zum Beispiel, die den Text undeutlich macht, ist auch eine reflektierende Fläche; während der Betrachter den Text entziffert, wirft ihm die Arbeit beständig sein eigenes Spiegelbild zurück. Die modernistische Obsession mit der Selbstreflexion bekommt hier eine ganz bestimmte Wendung; sie wird umgelenkt, zurückgeworfen auf den Betrachter, dessen Identität sich gleichzeitig in das Werk einschreibt.

Insofern *Baldwin # 4* Träger eines Zitats ist, widerlegt die Arbeit auch die Idee einer immanenten oder transzendenten Bedeutung. In der zitierten Passage aus James Baldwins Essayband *Teufelswerk* von 1976 (siehe den Beginn dieses Essays) entwirft Baldwin Identität als etwas *Extrinsisches*—ja Vorläufiges—und nicht Angeborenes, einem authentischen Selbst Innewohnendes. Unter diesem historisch bedingten "Gewand" liegt—wie ein Ei in seinem Nest—ein früheres, älteres Selbst, das (so wird jedenfalls impliziert) andere Identitäten, andere Formen annehmen kann.

Fast zwei Jahrzehnte nach ihrer Entstehung steckt in Baldwins lyrischer Formulierung noch immer eine ungeheure Brisanz, denn es ist eine offene Frage, ob Schwarze in Amerika so einfach "die Kleider wechseln", selbst für einen Moment nur ihre Hautfarbe vergessen können. Wie Drucilla Cornell berichtet, hat eine neuere Studie ergeben, daß "eine Person in den ersten *Sekunden* einer Begegnung zuerst nach der 'Rasse' dann nach dem 'Geschlecht' identifiziert wird".[13] Daß Ligon aus diesem utopischen Text ein *schwarzes* Gemälde macht, zumal in einem Schwarz, das den Text fast zudeckt, läßt auf

viewer, whose identity is simultaneously inscribed in the work.

Insofar as *Baldwin #4* is the bearer of a quotation, it also refutes the notion of immanent or transcendent meaning. In the quoted passage, excerpted from James Baldwin's 1976 *The Devil Finds Work* (see the opening page of this essay), Baldwin conceives identity as something *ex*trinsic—even provisional—rather than intrinsic to an innate and authentic self. Beneath this contingent "garment," like a nested egg, a prior and anterior selfhood may (or so it is implied) assume other identities, other avatars.

Almost two decades from its composition, Baldwin's lyric statement is charged with great poignancy, for it is an open question as to whether blacks in America are permitted so easily to "change robes," to forget, even momentarily, the mark of color. As Drucilla Cornell reports, a recent study has shown that "within the first *seconds* of an encounter, the viewed person is identified first by 'race' and then by 'sex'."[13] That Ligon makes of this utopian text a *black* painting, of a blackness, moreover, that almost submerges the text, suggests a counterproposition, namely the overwhelming determinations of race in America.

That the content of *Baldwin #4* is virtually invisible from any distance links it not only to other of Ligon's works that interrogate the dyads of whiteness/blackness and color/whiteness, but to one of the most pervasive thematics in the cultural production of writers and artists of color, a thematic, moreover, that figures prominently in *Mistaken Identities*. As indicated in the title of Michele Wallace's most recent book, *Invisibility Blues*, and searingly described at least as early as Ralph Ellison's *The Invisible Man* (1952), the social, psychic, and political consequences of invisibility are an infected wound in the very fabric of American life, which must now be confronted. To the belated and inculpating recognition that non-white Americans are in complex and mutually reinforcing ways rendered invisible within the spurious myth of the U.S. as a homogeneous, white, Anglo-Saxon culture, must be added the corollary acknowledgment that the invisibility of the black American has a particular and lethal aetiology. On the one hand, the mark of racial "blackness" operates to ratify the symbolic meanings of the word, with all its negative connotations of darkness, obscurity, and so forth. But on the other hand, there is a way that the mark of blackness functions to confer—

eine Gegendarstellung schließen, nämlich die der übermächtigen rassischen Determination in Amerika.

Daß der Inhalt von *Baldwin # 4* aus so gut wie jeder Distanz praktisch unsichtbar ist, verbindet das Bild nicht nur mit anderen Arbeiten Ligons, die sich mit den Begriffspaaren weiß/schwarz und farbig/weiß beschäftigen, sondern auch mit einem der durchgängigsten Themen in der Produktion farbiger Schriftsteller und Künstler, einer Thematik, die im übrigen auch in *Mistaken Identities* eine zentrale Rolle spielt. Wie im Titel des jüngsten Buchs von Michele Wallace, *Invisibility Blues,* angedeutet und wie mindestens schon in Ralph Ellisons *The Invisible Man* (1952) eindringlich beschrieben ist die soziale, psychische und politische Unsichtbarkeit eine schwärende Wunde mitten im Fleisch des amerikanischen Lebens, mit deren Folgen man sich nun auseinandersetzen muß. Die verspätete schuldbewußte Erkenntnis, daß nichtweiße Amerikaner auf vielfache und miteinander verschränkte Weisen innerhalb des falschen Mythos von den U.S.A. als einer homogenen, weißen, angelsächsischen Kultur unsichtbar gemacht wurden, muß durch die zusätzliche Erkenntnis ergänzt werden, daß die Unsichtbarkeit der schwarzen Amerikaner eine besondere—und letale—Ätiologie aufweist. Zum einen funktioniert das Mal des "Schwarzseins" als Bestätigung der symbolischen Bedeutungen des Worts mit all den negativen Obertönen des Finsteren, Dunklen, Obskuren usw.; andererseits aber verleiht es auch—nirgendwo verheerender als in der Wahrnehmung des jungen schwarzen Mannes—eine Art Hyper-Sichtbarkeit. Er wird damit zu einem leibhaftigen Totem der Bedrohung, zur Verkörperung von Gewalt und unerlaubter Sexualität schlechthin.[14]

Pat Ward Williams' *What you lookn at?* (Fig. 8) spricht diesen Widerspruch unmittelbar an. Ursprünglich geschaffen zur Installation in den Fenstern der Goldie Paley Gallery (am Moore College of Art and Design) und auf ähnliche Weise auch im Fenster des University Art Museums in Santa Barbara aufgestellt konfrontiert diese Foto-Text-Wand den Passanten mit den Abbildungen von fünf lebensgroßen jungen schwarzen Männern, die—frontal posierend—direkt auf die Straße hinausblicken. Obwohl objektiv gesehen nichts an ihnen auf eine besondere Bedrohung hinweist, geht die Arbeit von der Idee aus, daß der bloße Anblick solcher Jugendlicher für viele Leute beunruhigend und angsterregend ist.[15] Die Bildunterschrift im Grafittistil—"What you lookn at?"—mit ihrer argotartigen Schreibung und den klobigen Buchstaben—spielt mit den Konnotationen, für die Grafitti in den Augen der städtischen Bevölkerung häufig selbst stehen (Verfall der Stadt, Mißachtung von Eigentum, anarchische und

Fig. 8
Pat Ward Williams
What you lookn at?, 1992
Cat. no. 25

nowhere more damagingly than in the perception of the young black man—a kind of hyper-visibility; he thus becomes a veritable totem of menace, the very embodiment of violence and unlawful sexuality.[14]

Pat Ward Williams' *What you lookn at?* (fig. 8) speaks directly to this contradictory condition. Originally created for installation in the gallery windows of the Goldie Paley Gallery (Moore College of Art and Design) and similarly installed in the window of the University Art Museum, Santa Barbara, this photo-text mural confronts the passerby with life-size images of five young black men, frontally posed and looking directly out to the street. Although nothing about them objectively denotes any particular threat, the work is predicated on the notion that the mere sight of such youths is, for many people, disturbing and frightening.[15] The graffiti-type legend—"What you lookn at?"—in its argotic spelling as well as its crude lettering—battens on the signifieds of graffiti itself as it is often perceived by urban residents (e.g., the decay of the city, disrespect for property, anarchic and violent youth, etc.). But the interrogative "What you lookn at?" is, of course, hardly a neutral question. It is a challenge, a confrontation, a reproach. What you are looking at is in fact a menace as much fantasmatic as real. It is a collective bogey, variously comprising disavowal (a refusal of individual as well as political responsibility for the social production of criminality and violence); projection (individual and collective fantasies about what black men *are*); and anger and resentment (as people experience less and less control over the circumstances of their lives they tend to project their rage and anxiety on the scapegoated other).

Engaging this dense structure of projection and fantasy, Williams has manipulated her photographic image in such a way that as one approaches the surface, the figures lose resolution, decomposing into component particles. This dissolution has perhaps a utopian dimension; it is as though a closer confrontation with these racial phantoms reveals the viewer's own projective collusion. As Adrian Piper has remarked, "racism is a *visual* pathology," and one of the most compelling features of *What you lookn at?* is that it transforms the visceral, immediate trigger of racist response into a cautionary lesson, a heuristic brake on habitual and thus often unconscious forms of perception.

Furthermore, that *What you lookn at?* was designed for display in a gallery or museum window prompts another level of meaning, insofar as the window

gewalttätige Jugendliche usw.). Aber die Frage *What you lookn at?* ist natürlich alles andere als neutral. Sie ist eine Herausforderung, eine Konfrontation, ein Vorwurf. Was man tatsächlich sieht, ist eine Bedrohung, die nicht weniger phantasmatisch als real ist—ein kollektiver Buhmann zusammengesetzt aus Verleugnung (der Verweigerung individueller wie politischer Verantwortung für die gesellschaftliche Produktion von Kriminalität und Gewalt), aus Projektion (den individuellen und kollektiven Phantasien über das Wesen schwarzer Männer) sowie aus Ärger und Ressentiment (die mit dem allmählichen Verlust der Kontrolle über ihre Lebensumstände einhergehende Tendenz der Menschen, ihre Wut und Angst auf den zum Sündenbock gestempelten anderen zu projizieren).

Dieses dichte Gewebe aus Projektion und Phantasie aufgreifend hat Williams die fotografische Darstellung so manipuliert, daß die Figuren mit der Annäherung an das Bild an Entschlossenheit verlieren, sich in ihre Bestandteile auflösen. Diese Auflösung hat vielleicht eine utopische Dimension; es ist, als würde die nähere Konfrontation mit diesen Rassenphantomen die voreingenommene Projektion des Betrachters selbst enthüllen. Adrian Piper hat einmal bemerkt: "Rassismus ist ein Sehfehler". Es ist eine der bemerkenswertesten Eigenschaften von *What you lookn at?*, daß es der instinktiven, unmittelbaren rassistischen Reaktion eine mahnende Lektion erteilt, den gewohnheitsmäßigen und damit oft unbewußten Wahrnehmungsweisen eine heuristische Bremse vorsetzt.

Die Tatsache, daß *What you lookn at?* für die Ausstellung in einem Galerie- oder Museumsfenster konzipiert ist, bringt aber noch eine weitere Bedeutungsebene ins Spiel, ist doch das Fenster normalerweise der "öffentlichste" Raum eines Museums, Trennlinie zwischen dem Heiligtum der Elitekultur und der Heterogenität der Straße. Durch die Besetzung dieses Zwischenraums macht das an den Passanten "gerichtete" Bild junger schwarzer Männer deutlich, daß deren exzessive Sichtbarkeit—eine Sichtbarkeit, die aber nichts mit gegenseitiger Anerkennung oder Zuneigung zu tun hat—die primäre Form ist, in der schwarze (männliche) Jugendliche öffentliche Aufmerksamkeit erregen.

Im Gegensatz zur ominösen Hypersichtbarkeit junger schwarzer Männer geht es in den Arbeiten Lorna Simpsons vornehmlich, wenn nicht sogar grundlegend, um die diskursive Unsichtbarkeit schwarzer Frauen. Wenn es auch stimmt daß—wie Michele Wallace argumentiert hat—schwarze Frauen in der zeitgenössischen amerikanischen Kultur auch das Objekt einer erhöhten (und massiv fetischisierten) Sichtbarkeit sein können, wie in gewissen Bereichen der Unterhaltungs- und Musikindustrie, so existiert diese Sichtbarkeit doch in der

Fig. 9
Lorna Simpson
Dividing Lines, 1989
Cat. no. 17

line one's pocket | actor's lines | same ol' line | out of line

silver lining | red lining | line - up | color line

is normally the most "public" space of the museum, dividing the sanctum of elite culture from the heterogeneity of the street. Occupying this liminal space, the image of young black men "addressed" to passersby suggests that their excessive visibility—a visibility which has nonetheless nothing to do with mutual recognition or affective reciprocity—is the principal form in which black (male) youth achieves public recognition.

In contrast to the ominous hypervisibility of young black men, much of Lorna Simpson's work has been preoccupied with, if not predicated on, the discursive invisibility of black women. While it is true, as Michele Wallace has argued, that in contemporary American culture black women may also be the object of a heightened (and intensely fetishized) visibility, as in certain segments of the entertainment or music industry, this visibility exists for the most part within the presiding terms of spectacle. The highly mediated "presence" of a few black women performers is by no means a corrective, or even an equalizer of the non-place to which most women of color have been historically relegated. This is an invisibility that greatly exceeds the boundaries of metaphor, encompassing as it does the erasure of black women from history, indeed, from American culture itself—the occulting of black female subjectivity across the board, even including black women's invisibility within oppositional and liberation movements (e.g., civil rights, Black power, feminism, etc.).

Hauptsache unter den kontrollierten Bedingungen des Spektakels. Die hochvermittelte "Präsenz" einiger weniger schwarzer Schauspielerinnen und Sängerinnen ist bei weitem kein Korrektiv oder gar Ausgleich für den Un-Ort, an den die meisten schwarzen Frauen historisch verbannt wurden. Diese charakteristische Unsichtbarkeit geht über das Metaphorische weit hinaus, bedeutet sie doch die Streichung schwarzer Frauen aus der Geschichte, ja überhaupt aus der amerikanischen Kultur—die Ausblendung des schwarzen weiblichen Subjekts auf allen Ebenen, selbst in den Oppositions- und Befreiungsbewegungen (wie Bürgerrechtsbewegung, Black-Power-Bewegung, Feminismus usw.)

Simpsons idealtypische schwarze Frau, obwohl in Bedeutung und Funktion von Werk zu Werk verschieden, ist stets ein Andenken an diese historische und diskursive Repression. Kopflos, gesichtslos oder vom Betrachter abgewandt verkörpert sie ihre Auslöschung zugleich mit der Etablierung ihrer Präsenz. Diese Weigerung, das Bild der Frau voll dem Betrachter auszuliefern, weist gewisse Ähnlichkeiten mit dem feministischen Ikonoklasmus Mary Kellys auf, spielt aber auch eine spezifische Rolle in Simpsons gesamtem Werk. Wie ihre Verwendung elliptischer und fragmentarischer Wörter und Wendungen, deren Assoziationen und Bedeutungen der Betrachter mit Sinn füllen muß, ist diese Fragmentierung und Auslöschung der schwarzen Frau ein Generator von Bedeutungen und nicht deren unveränderliches Aufnahmegefäß.[16]

Simpsons gesichtslose Frau ist tatsächlich eine Art visuelle Chiffre. Ob jung oder ältlich, hübsch oder unscheinbar—

Fig. 10a–b
Mary Kelly
Menacé (one of three diptychs)
from *Corpus*, 1984–85
Cat. no. 7

the room is crowded yet subdued, almost silent. No music,
no dancing. Everyone is talking quietly in couples or small
groups. Many are old friends, some I haven't seen for
several years. They look different, not just greyer or fatter
or more degenerate or less fashionable, just not the same.
We are celebrating Lynn's fortieth birthday. "You look
great," she says kissing me on both cheeks, "haven't
changed at all," then Anna mocks us but affectionately,
"well preserved." She smiles. We laugh. I am content. I bask
in the warmth, the comfort of their compliments, im-
mutable, at least until Rod whispers, "How old are you anyway?"
and I remember I am nearly forty-three. I hesitate and Sarah
fills the gap with, "See, she can't even say it." A possible re-
prieve, Elizabeth, comes over and asks me what I'm working
on. I tell her it's another long project and hope she won't
pursue it. "On what," she insists. I fumble, knowing it will
sound dreadful no matter how I say it, "middle-age, well
that is, I suppose I mean women like us." "I don't feel middle-
aged," she snaps, seems offended. I try to explain that it's not
so literal, more about the way we represent it to ourselves,
almost before the fact. She says she has a phobia about it,
tries to change the subject. Sarah interrupts to tell me the
leather jacket is lovely but she distinctly remembers that
I said I'd never wear one. I confess I finally gave in for
professional reasons, that there's so much to think about
now besides what to wear, that the older you are the harder
it seems to be to get it right and that the uniform makes
it a little easier. I look at Maya for confirmation but she
disagrees, says there's a certain freedom attached to getting
older, not caring so much, being able to get up in the
morning and get dressed like a man, confidently, without
wasting time primping. I notice she is dressed simply, hair
hanging loosely on her shoulders, wearing very little make-up,
nearly sixty and absolutely gorgeous. I say I'm not so sure
most men are that secure but maybe her confidence comes
from knowing she has always been a very attractive
woman. She looks surprised. "No one is that confident,"
she protests, "I must admit I've never missed an opportunity
to glance in a mirror as I passed it, or in a shop window
or any reflective surface for that matter, hoping to catch
a glimpse of myself as others see me." Lynn is lighting the
candles. "Watch me," she says, "I'm going to blow them out now."
And one does, all forty, without a flicker.

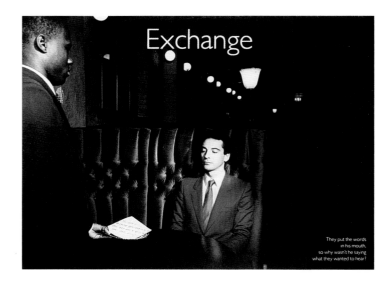

Fig. 11a–c
Mitra Tabrizian and Andy Golding
The Blues, 1986–87
(third of three triptychs)
Cat. no 21

Simpson's generic black woman, despite the shift in her meaning and function from work to work, always commemorates this historical and discursive repression. Headless, faceless, or turned away from the spectator, she simultaneously enacts her effacement while instituting her presence. While this refusal to fully deliver the image of the woman to the viewer bears certain resemblances to the feminist iconoclasm of Mary Kelly, it also plays a distinctive role within Simpson's work as a whole. Like her use of elliptical and fragmentary words and phrases whose meanings and associations must be given significance by the viewer, this fragmented and effaced black woman is a generator of meaning(s), not a stable receptacle for them.[16]

Simpson's faceless woman is, in fact, a kind of visual cipher. Whether young or middle-aged, pretty or plain, in the decontextualized space of the seamless backdrop she is merely a graphic assertion of black femaleness. Hence, it is the work of language to quicken and animate this static marker of racial and sexual difference.

In a work such as *Dividing Lines* (fig. 9), a selection of myriad applications of the word "lines" suffices to mobilize the image, galvanizing a set of meanings that range from the economic ("line one's pocket," "red lining"—e.g., the banking practice of refusing mortgages in low income neighborhoods); to the transgressive ("out of line," "line up"); to the mendaciousness of language ("same ol' line"); ending with the unambiguously racial "color line."

Simpson's linguistic plays, no matter how polysemic or deliberately ambiguous, are always played off

in dem entkontextualisierten Raum des glatten Hintergrunds ist sie bloß eine bildliche Behauptung schwarzer Weiblichkeit. Es wird daher Aufgabe der Sprache, dieses statische Zeichen rassischer und geschlechtlicher Differenz lebendig werden zu lassen.

In einer Arbeit wie *Dividing Lines* (Fig. 9) genügt eine bestimmte Auswahl aus den unzähligen Verwendungsweisen des Wortes "line", um das Bild in Bewegung zu setzen und eine Reihe von Bedeutungen zu induzieren, die vom ökonomischen ("line one's pocket"—sich die Taschen füllen; "red lining"—die Praxis der Banken, in Vierteln mit geringem Einkommen keine Hypotheken zu vergeben) über die Überschreitung ("out of line"—aus der Reihe tanzen; "line up"—sich zusammenschließen) und die Verlogenheit der Sprache ("same ol' line"—dieselbe alte Leier) bis zur schließlich unzweideutig rassisch gemeinten "color line" reichen.

Simpsons Sprachspiele, wie polysemisch oder bewußt uneindeutig sie auch sein mögen, werden stets gegen die enigmatische An-/Abwesenheit ihres schwarzen Modells ausgespielt. Der Betrachter ist so dazu gezwungen, über die möglichen Beziehungen zwischen einer anonymen farbigen Frau—einem Körper, irgendeinem Körper—und den politischen, sozialen und häufig geschlechtlichen Assoziationen ihrer Texte nachzudenken. Und trotz der schönen, anschaulichen und sogar verführerischen Präsentation ihrer Arbeiten könnte man die herausfordernde Weigerung, die Frau dem Blick des Betrachters preiszugeben, als eine weitere strategische Möglichkeit sehen, mit Pipers Diagnose "Rassismus ist ein Sehfehler" umzugehen.

Sofern sich Simpsons Werk ebensosehr mit dem Geschlecht wie mit der Rasse auseinandersetzt, ist festzustellen,

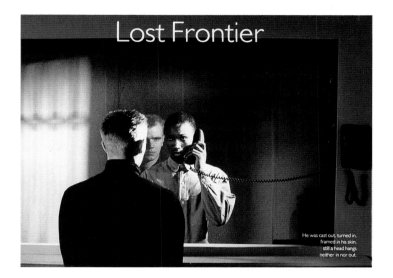

against the enigmatic presence/absence of her black model. The viewer is therefore enjoined to reflect upon the possible relations between an anonymous woman of color—a body, as in "any body"—and the political, social, and often sexual associations of her texts. And despite the handsome, graphic, even seductive presentation of her works, the tantalizing refusal to proffer the woman to the viewer's gaze may be thought of as yet another stratagem of response to Piper's "racism is a *visual* pathology."

To the extent, moreover, that Simpson's work engages gender as often as race, it must be acknowledged that the representation of femininity, black and white, is inescapably moored in dynamics of fetishism, voyeurism and (male) fantasies of mastery, possession, and imaginary knowledge. Pathologies of the visual are by no means limited to the operations of racism. Insofar as women may be said to constitute a subaltern group within patriarchy, and insofar as issues of visibility/invisibility impact in quite specific ways on feminine identity, Mary Kelly's *Corpus* (fig. 10a–b) resonates in interesting ways with Simpson's work. The inclusion of an excerpt from Kelly's *Interim* is thus consistent with the themes of the exhibition as a whole. Whereas the monumental *Interim* in its entirety investigates the problematic identity of the aging white, middle-class woman, paralleled by the historical fortunes of modern feminism, both of which are indexed to the social and economic status of women, *Corpus* is the section most concerned with the problematics of visibility. A woman's experience of aging is here understood as deeply implicated in such problematics, since one of the

daß die Repräsentation von Weiblichkeit—ob schwarz oder weiß—unentwirrbar mit der Dynamik von Fetischismus, Voyeurismus und (männlichen) Phantasien von Macht, Besitz und imaginärem Wissen verquickt ist. Sehfehler sind keineswegs nur auf den Rassismus beschränkt. Soweit man sagen kann, daß Frauen eine subalterne Gruppe innerhalb des Patriarchats darstellen und soweit Fragen der Sichtbarkeit/Unsichtbarkeit auch ganz bestimmte Auswirkungen auf die weibliche Identität haben, überschneidet sich Mary Kellys *Corpus* (Fig. 10a–b) auf interessante Weise mit der Arbeit Simpsons. Die Aufnahme dieses Teils aus Kellys *Interim* fügt sich damit in die Themen der gesamten Ausstellung ein. Während die monumentale Arbeit *Interim* als Ganzes die problematische Identität der alternden weißen Mittelschichtfrau untersucht und parallel dazu die historischen Geschicke des modernen Feminismus—beides unter Hinweis auf den sozialen und ökonomischen Status von Frauen—ist *Corpus* jener Teil, der sich am meisten mit der Problematik der Sichtbarkeit beschäftigt. Das Altern der Frau ist eng mit dieser Problematik verbunden, da eine der Aporien der Weiblichkeit darin besteht, daß die Sichtbarkeit von Frauen schwindet, wenn sie die Reproduktionsfähigkeit überschreiten und unweigerlich in den (kulturell produzierten) sexuellen Limbus des Alters abgedrängt werden.

Aber während ein Aspekt der Repression weiblicher Identität in verschiedenen Formen der Unsichtbarkeit besteht (enkodiert zum Beispiel in sprachlichen Ausdrücken wie "Mannschaft"), ergeben sich andere genau umgekehrt durch eine exzessive Betonung des Visuellen (wenn auch in anderer Weise als im Fall der jungen schwarzen Männer).[17] So vermeinte zum Beispiel die Medizin des neunzehnten Jahrhunderts die Zeichen geistiger und körperlicher Minderwertigkeit

aporias of femininity lies in the eclipse of visibility as women pass beyond the age of reproductive capability and are inexorably moved toward the (culturally imposed) sexual limbo of old age.

But where one oppressive aspect of feminine identity is constructed through various forms of invisibility (encoded, for example, in linguistic usage such as "mankind"), others are bred precisely through an excessive emphasis on the visual (although differently inflected from the way this functions in the case of young black men).[17] Nineteenth-century medical science, for example, professed to read the signs of mental and physical inferiority *visually* from the appearance or the morphology of women. In this regard, Kelly's *Corpus* makes pointed reference to the late nineteenth-century French discourse of hysteria. Codified by Dr. Jean Martin Charcot and quite literally enacted by the incarcerated women at the Parisian hospital of Salpétrière, hysteria was preeminently a visual, not to say spectacular malady.

In evoking hysteria's putative phases and "events," (the *attitudes passionelles*), Kelly mobilizes but one of her historical motifs. Orchestrated too within *Corpus* is a handwritten fiction of contemporary white feminine subjectivity, consisting of reveries, daily incidents, reflections, and anxieties, many of which revolve around the more or less subtle experiences that constitute the perception of aging. These text panels are themselves counterpointed with images of apparel—shoes, leather jacket, nightgown—photographically reproduced in such a way as to appear simultaneously concrete and illusionistic, material and spectral. Participating in both the (a)logic of the commodity and the psychic fetish, and lastly, as a metonym for the body itself, *Corpus* reminds us that the conditions and constraints of feminine identity, like all others, are generated fully as much by the social and political as by the psychic.

The attempt to encompass all three of these fields of identity as they constitute the "alchemy" of race[18] also structures the three triptychs that make up Mitra Tabrizian and Andy Golding's *The Blues* (fig. 11a–c). A collaboration between a London-based Iranian woman and an English man, this is the only work by non-American artists in the exhibition. Created between the years 1986–1987, *The Blues* is especially significant as a work exploring the intersections of race and gender. That *The Blues* was produced as a collaboration between non-black artists is itself significant.[19] Years ago, I remember seeing Tabrizian

visuell—am Aussehen und der Morphologie von Frauen—ablesen zu können. Kellys *Corpus* nimmt gezielt Bezug auf den französischen Hysteriediskurs des neunzehnten Jahrhunderts. Die Hysterie, wie sie von Dr. Jean Martin Charcot kodifiziert und von den Insassinnen der Salpétrière in Paris im wahrsten Sinne verkörpert wurde, war ein eminent visuelles, um nicht zu sagen spektakuläres Leiden.

Mit dem Bezug auf die vermeintlichen Phasen und "Ereignisse" der Hysterie (die *attitudes passionnelles*) mobilisiert Kelly aber nur eines ihrer historischen Motive. Daneben wird in *Corpus* eine fiktives handgeschriebenes Dokument zeitgenössischer weißer weiblicher Subjektivität entfaltet—bestehend aus Träumen, täglichen Geschehnissen, Reflexionen und Ängsten, von denen viele mehr oder weniger subtil um die Erfahrung des Alterns kreisen. Diese Texttafeln werden ihrerseits kontrastiert mit Bildern von Kleidungsstücken—Schuhe, Lederjacke, Nachthemd—, deren fotografische Reproduktion sie gleichzeitig konkret und illusionistisch, stofflich und geisterhaft erscheinen läßt. Sowohl an der (A)logik der Ware wie des psychischen Fetisch teilhabend und letztlich ein Metonym für den Körper selbst erinnert uns *Corpus* daran, daß die Bedingungen und Beschränkungen weiblicher Identität—wie jeder anderen auch—genausosehr durch das Soziale und Politische wie durch das Psychische erzeugt werden.

Der Versuch, diese drei die "Alchimie" der Rasse[18] konstituierenden Felder der Identität miteinander zu verbinden, kennzeichnet auch die drei Triptychen, aus denen Mitra Tabrizians und Andy Goldings *The Blues* (Fig. 11a–c) besteht. Diese Gemeinschaftsarbeit einer in London lebenden Iranerin und eines Engländers ist die einzige Arbeit nichtamerikanischer Künstler in der Ausstellung. Entstanden zwischen 1986 und 1987 ist *The Blues* besonders signifikant als eine Arbeit, die die Kreuzungen von Rasse und Geschlecht untersucht. Ebenso bedeutsam ist es, daß eine solche Arbeit von einer Iranerin und einem weißen Briten produziert wurde.[19] Ich erinnere mich an einen Vortrag Tabrizians in New York, bei dem sie diese Arbeit präsentierte und wo sie wütend von jemandem aus dem Publikum wegen der Anmaßung angegriffen wurde, als Weiße die Darstellung von Schwarzen zu "psychoanalysieren". Ihre erste Reaktion—"Rassismus ist ein Problem für *Weiße*"—ist tatsächlich ein prägendes Prinzip dieser Arbeit, die sich um die intrasubjektiven Mechanismen von Rasse und Rassismus, Geschlecht und Sexualität dreht.

Wie die meisten Kunstwerke dieser Ausstellung läßt sich *The Blues* nicht auf einen knappen, summarischen Nenner bringen. Neben der Anspielung des Titels auf Melancholie und eine bestimmte Form schwarzer Kultur greift *The*

present this work at a talk she gave in New York City, where she was angrily challenged by a member of the audience for presuming, as a white woman, to "psychoanalyze" representations of black people. Her immediate response—"Racism is a problem for *white* people"—is actually an informing principle of this work, which turns on the intrasubjective mechanisms of race and racism, gender and sexuality.

Like much of the art in this exhibition, *The Blues* does not lend itself to capsule summary or thumbnail exegesis. With its titular allusion to melancholy and to a distinctive form of black culture, *The Blues* also draws on conventions of cinema (e.g., film noir—itself a pun); high art (e.g., the image labelled *The Interior* is a reworking of Degas' *The Interior*, also known as *The Rape*); and hard-boiled detective novels. Staged as a series of *tableaux vivants*, images and texts combine to solicit the viewer's fantasies about the "role" of black men and women within scenarios suggestive of murder or suicide, aggression, political confrontation, abjection. Often, the black protagonists are the psychological and physical locus of the gaze of white men. Alternatively, white men are presented as aggressively threatening or twinned with the black men. In one tableau, the black woman appears as an active agent (thereby reversing the role of the passive woman in the Degas); in another, she is dead; a third features a masked white woman, looming above the seated, white-masked black. The implied narrative or the role of the women in *The Blues* signals the complicated (and often repressed) role of gender within the matrices of race, masculinity, and interracial relations between men. Whose stories, we may ask, are these? In fact, and for all its density of reference to mass-cultural forms, *The Blues* is constructed along lines analogous to Freudian dreamwork, deploying strategies of displacement, condensation, and considerations of representability (hence, the punning use of language).[20] The use of mirrors, windows, and reflective surfaces further insinuates the psychic, interiorized space in which the confrontations of self and other are staged and invested with meaning.

Implicit in the psychoanalytically informed work of Kelly and of Tabrizian and Golding is the conviction that the formation of individual identity, as well as beliefs about the other's identity, are jointly forged by unconscious processes that are more or less inaccessible to logic, reason, or empirical revision. This immediately raises the political question of how art practices that are obviously

Blues auch auf Kinokonventionen (z.B. den filme noir—selbst ein Wortspiel), Hochkunst (das Bild mit dem Titel *The Interior* ist z.B. eine Bearbeitung von Degas' *Intérieur*, auch als *Die Vergewaltigung* bekannt) und hartgesottene Detektivromane zurück. Angelegt als eine Serie von *tableaux vivants* sind die Bilder und Texte so kombiniert, daß sie die Phantasien des Betrachters über die "Rolle" schwarzer Männer in Mord oder Selbstmord, Aggression, politischer Konfrontation und Verzweiflung suggerierenden Szenarios anregen. Sehr oft stehen die schwarzen Protagonisten psychologisch und physisch im Blickpunkt weißer Männer. Hingegen werden weiße Männer entweder als aggressiv bedrohlich oder gepaart mit schwarzen Männern dargestellt. Auf einem Tableau erscheint die schwarze Frau als die aktiv Handelnde (womit die Rolle der passiven Frau bei Degas umgekehrt wird); auf einem anderen Tableau ist sie tot; ein drittes zeigt eine maskierte weiße Frau, die auf einen sitzenden weißmaskierten Schwarzen hinabblickt. Die Position oder Narration der Frauen in *The Blues* signalisiert die komplizierte (und oft verdrängte) Rolle des Geschlechts in den Schablonen von Rasse, Männlichkeit und Männerbeziehungen. Wessen Geschichten, könnten wir uns fragen, sind das? Tatsächlich—und trotz all seiner vielfältigen Bezüge auf die Massenkultur—ist *The Blues* nach Prinzipien konstruiert, die der Freudschen Traumarbeit analog sind, es werden Verschiebungs- und Verdichtungsstrategien benutzt und Überlegungen zur Darstellbarkeit angestellt (daher der spielerische Umgang mit Sprache).[20] Die Verwendung von Spiegeln, Fenstern und reflektierenden Oberflächen suggeriert zusätzlich den psychischen, verinnerlichten Raum, in dem die Begegnung von Selbst und Anderem in Szene gesetzt und mit Bedeutung erfüllt wird.

Den psychoanalytisch geprägten Arbeiten von Kelly, Tabrizian und Golding liegt die implizite Überzeugung zugrunde, daß die Formation individueller Identität wie auch der Ansichten über die Identität des anderen durch das Zusammenwirken unbewußter Prozesse erfolgt, zu denen Logik, Vernunft oder empirische Revisionen keinen Zugang haben. Eine solche Position wirft natürlich sofort die politische Frage auf: Wie sollen künstlerische Praktiken, die offensichtlich der Analyse von Sexismus und Rassismus verpflichtet und damit politisch motiviert sind, tiefverwurzelte Einstellungen und Überzeugungen beeinflussen—und verändern? Ungelöst bleibt natürlich für *alle* kritischen und politischen Kunstpraktiken (vor allem für jene, die sich innerhalb der Grenzen der Elitekultur bewegen), wie sie die gewünschten Interventionen und Transformationen in die Tat umsetzen können. Sofern Kunstwerke—selbst die allerkonzeptuellsten—sowohl im

Fig. 12a
Connie Hatch
briefing sheet for "Unknown Woman" from
Some Americans: Forced to Disappear, 1990–91
Cat. no. 4

committed to an analysis of sexism and racism, and thus motivated by political concerns, are to act upon—to transform—entrenched attitudes and beliefs. It remains, of course, unresolved for *all* critical and political art practices (particularly those that exist within the confines of elite culture) as to how to effect their desired interventions and transformations. To the degree that art objects, even the most rigorously conceptual, operate to mobilize non-rational, pre-conscious and unconscious responses in both artist *and* spectator, one could argue that it is precisely along the lines of the psychic and fantasmatic that critical art practice operates most potently. The more purely *political* valencies of identity may, however, require their own forms of analysis; thus, while some artists in *Mistaken Identities* construct their work to mobilize relatively fluid associative trains, others, like Connie Hatch, are closer to the tradition of heuristic political art exemplified by artists like Hans Haacke and Krzysztof Wodiczko.

In Hatch's *Some Americans: Forced to Disappear* (fig. 12a–b), derived from the larger project entitled *A Display of Visual Inequity*, the structuring terms of visibility/invisibility are again at issue. Hatch is here concerned with the circumstances and determinations by which some individuals are "recognized" (literally, by the spectator, and more generally, by the culture at large) and others relegated to obscurity and anonymity. All of the American women (and the one man) whose portraits are mounted on the wall have disappeared—died—under known or unknown circumstances. "Identity" is

Künstler wie auch im Betrachter nichtrationale, vor- und unbewußte Reaktionsweisen auslösen, könnte man behaupten, daß kritische Kunstpraktiken gerade auf der Ebene des Psychischen und Phantasmatischen am wirksamsten sind. Die im strengeren Sinn *politischen* Valenzen der Identität dürften indessen ihre eigenen Analyseformen erfordern. Während also einige Künstler in *Mistaken Identities* mit ihren Arbeiten relativ freie Assoziationsabläufe in Gang setzen, sind andere—wie Connie Hatch—stärker der Tradition einer heuristischen Politkunst verbunden, wie sie durch Künstler wie Hans Haacke oder Krzysztof Wodiczko exemplifiziert wird.

In Hatchs Arbeit *Some Americans: Forced to Disappear* (Fig. 12a–b), die aus dem größeren Projekt *A Display of Visual Inequity* entwickelt wurde, sind wiederum die strukturierenden Begriffe Sichtbarkeit/ Unsichtbarkeit am Werk. Hatch geht es in dieser Arbeit um die Umstände und Bedingungen, unter denen manche Personen "(an)erkannt" (im buchstäblichen Sinn, erkannt vom Betrachter, und allgemeiner, anerkannt von der Kultur insgesamt), während andere in die Anonymität verbannt und übersehen werden. Die amerikanischen Frauen, deren Porträts an der Wand montiert sind, sind alle unter bekannten oder unbekannten Umständen verschwunden—gestorben. "Identität" wird in dieser Arbeit als etwas ganz und gar sozial, ja politisch Produziertes behandelt, als etwas, das im Fall eines berühmten Kinostars—wie Marilyn Monroe—maximale Sichtbarkeit erlangt und maximale Unsichtbarkeit im Fall der Opfer offizieller oder auch bloß zufälliger Gewalt (wie die unbekannte Japano-Amerikanerin, die im U.S.-Internierungslager während des Zweiten Weltkriegs "das letzte Mal gesehen" wurde; das "verschwundene" Kind,

Fig. 12b
Connie Hatch
"Unknown Woman" from *Some Americans:*
Forced to Disappear, 1990–91
Cat. no. 4

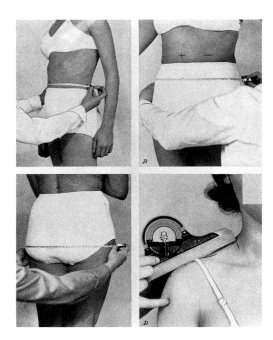

Fig. 13
Martha Rosler
video stills from *Vital Statistics of
a Citizen. Simply Obtained,* 1978
Cat. no. 30

approached in this work as a fully social and indeed political production, one that achieves maximum visibility in
the case of a famous movie star, such as Marilyn Monroe,
and maximum invisibility in the case of victims of official,
or merely arbitrary violence (e.g., the unknown Japanese-
American woman "last seen" when interned in the U.S.
detention camp during World War II; the "disappeared"
child whose image comes from the reverse side of a carpet
cleaning advertisement; the Argentine woman "disappeared" during the counter-insurgency operations of the
Argentine junta). Confronted with the wall of portraits
mounted and lit in such a way as to produce a ghostly
double on the surface of the wall, the spectator normally
recognizes some, but not most of the faces. On an adja-
cent wall, however, Hatch affixes what she calls briefing
sheets, which provide the identifying biographical information and the circumstances (when known) of the
subject's disappearance. Written in a style that mimics the
source of her information (news magazines, popular biog-
raphy, history books, etc.), the aggregate effect of the texts
is to foster consideration of the political valencies of identity, whereby the brute fact of having been born female
rather than male, black rather than white, Japanese-Amer-
ican in wartime America, and so forth, are in and of themselves determinations that override the particularities of
individual identity.

The political components of identity are also the
subject of Martha Rosler's videotape, *Vital Statistics of a*

dessen Bild von der Rückseite einer Werbung für Teppichreini-
gungsmittel stammt; die argentinische Frau, die während der
Anti-Aufruhr-Maßnahmen der argentinischen Junta
"verschwand"). Der Betrachter, der auf die Porträts blickt, die
so montiert und beleuchtet sind, daß an der Wand geisterhafte
Doubles entstehen, erkennt in der Regel einige der Gesichter,
die meisten aber nicht. An einer angrenzenden Wand bringt
Hatch jedoch sogenannte "Instruktionen" an, die die zur Iden-
tifikation notwendigen biographischen Angaben und (falls
bekannt) auch Informationen über die Umstände des
Verschwindens der Personen liefern. In einem die Informa-
tionsquellen (Nachrichtenmagazine, Starbiographien,
Geschichtsbücher usw.) imitierenden Stil verfaßt fördern diese
Texte in ihrer Gesamtwirkung eine Betrachtung der politischen
Komponenten von Identität, wobei die nackte Tatsache, daß
jemand als Frau statt als Mann, als Schwarze statt als Weiße,
als Japano-Amerikanerin während des Krieges usw. zur Welt
gekommen ist, allein schon so determinierend ist, daß sie die
Besonderheiten der individuellen Identität überlagert.

Die politischen Komponenten der Identität sind auch
Gegenstand von Martha Roslers Videoarbeit, *Vital Statistics of
a Citizen, Simply Obtained* (Fig. 13), in der ein weibliches
Subjekt klinisch und leidenschaftslos untersucht, gewogen,
gemessen und entkleidet wird. Als Subjekt (Bürger *und* Unter-
tan) eines panoptischen Staates—und implizit aller modernen
Staaten—unterwirft sich Roslers namenlose Frau einem
Prozeß, der eine allegorische Verkörperung von Michel
Foucaults Analyse der Allianz von Wissen und Macht darstellt.
Wir werden so daran erinnert, daß hinter dieser alptraumhaf-
ten Vermessung eines einzelnen Körpers unser aller tägliche
Wirklichkeit der bürokratischen Maßnahmen, der Ausweise,
Pässe, Krankenhausberichte liegt—: all der Methoden, mit
denen unser Körper erfaßt und aufgezeichnet und damit unter-
worfen wird. Die Tatsache, daß dieses Subjekt weiblich ist, hat
aber noch weitere Konnotationen—Konnotationen, auf die
auch Kellys Arbeit verweist. Spätestens seit dem neunzehnten
Jahrhundert hat der weibliche Körper am stärksten den Blick
des Wissens/der Macht auf sich gezogen, war es der weibliche
Körper, an dem sich entzündete, was Foucault den "Wahn des
Sichtbaren" nennt. Dementsprechend betont Rosler, daß das
Aus- und Vermessen des weiblichen Körpers eine spezifische
Bedeutung der Weiblichkeit behält.

Sofern man Identität als ein Amalgam von inneren
und äußeren Determinanten sehen kann, besteht eine gewisse
Versuchung, erstere dem Bereich des Psychischen und letztere
dem Bereich des Sozialen zuzuordnen. In Wirklichkeit sind
solche Unterscheidungen unhaltbar. So findet zum Beispiel die

Citizen, Simply Obtained (fig. 13), in which a female subject is clinically and dispassionately surveyed, weighed, measured, and stripped. Subject *of* and subject *to* a Panoptic state—by implication, all modern states—Rosler's unnamed woman submits to a process that is a veritable allegorization of Michel Foucault's analysis of the twinned alignments of knowledge and power. We are thus reminded that behind this nightmarish mapping and measuring of an individual body lies the real-life actuality of bureaucratic procedures, identity cards, passports, hospital records, all the appurtenances by which the body is known and recorded, becoming thereby a subjected body. That this subject is female has an additional set of connotations, signalled as well in Kelly's work. At least since the nineteenth century, it has been the female body that most provokes the gaze of knowledge/power, the body that excites what Foucault called "the frenzy of the visible." Accordingly, Rosler emphasizes that the measuring and mapping of the female body has specific meaning with respect to the ideological construction of femininity.

Insofar as identity can be viewed as an amalgam of both interior and exterior determinations, there is some temptation to ascribe the former to the realm of the psychic and the latter to the realm of the social. In fact, such distinctions are untenable. For example, the formation of sexual subjectivity is forged in infancy and early childhood, in the family, in the individual psyche. Nevertheless, the significance *attributed* to sexual difference is consequent upon the differential values accorded the biological fact of being male or female—values that are, moreover, determined by the symbolic order of patriarchy, which is a social form *anterior* to its individual psychic assimilation. Similarly, "race," to the degree that it has any biological and scientifically valid status at all (and that is little enough), has meaning only by virtue of the social and political implications that accompany its ascription. Yet its significance, though thoroughly adventitious and primarily social, is nonetheless psychically assimilated, becoming, in racist cultures or contexts, as inescapable and devastating a fact of psychic life as it is of social life. Accordingly, race is both a chimera and a social reality, making it an especially intractable object for critical art practice. Furthermore, to the extent that racism may be quite unconscious, harbored even despite one's moral and ethical convictions, art production that confronts it in its more covert incarnations must necessarily operate on several fronts.

Konstitution der geschlechtlichen Identität in der frühen Kindheit, in der Familie, in der Psyche des Individuums statt, aber der der Geschlechtsdifferenz zugeschriebene Sinn folgt aus der unterschiedlichen Bewertung der biologischen Tatsache des Mann- oder Frauseins—einer Bewertung, die durch die symbolische Ordnung des Patriarchats determiniert ist, das seinerseits eine soziale Form ist, die ihrer individuellen psychischen Assimilation *vorausgeht*. Auf ähnliche Weise erhält "Rasse", sofern ihr überhaupt ein biologisch oder wissenschaftlich gültiger Status zukommt (und der ist eher gering), einen Sinn erst aufgrund der sozialen und politischen Implikationen, die mit einer solchen Zuschreibung einhergehen. Aber dieser Sinn, obwohl durch und durch akzidentell und in erster Linie sozial, wird dennoch psychisch assimiliert und wird in rassistischen Kulturen oder Kontexten nichtsdestoweniger zu einem unentrinnbaren und zerstörerischen Faktum des psychischen und sozialen Lebens. Demnach ist Rasse sowohl eine Chimäre als auch soziale Realität, was sie zu einem besonders schwer greifbaren Objekt kritischer Kunstpraxis macht. Sofern Rassismus überdies etwas völlig Unbewußtes sein kann—gehegt gegen die eigenen moralischen und ethischen Überzeugungen—, muß die künstlerische Praxis, die sich mit seinen verborgeneren Manifestationen auseinandersetzt, notgedrungen auf verschiedenen Fronten operieren.

In dieser Hinsicht ist Adrian Pipers Videoinstallation *Cornered* (Fig. 14) eine besonders wichtige Arbeit, die uneingestandene oder unbemerkte Rassismen provoziert, während sie gleichzeitig eine elegante Dekonstruktion des amerikanischen kulturellen *Mythos* von Weiß und Schwarz vornimmt. Selbst eine hellhäutige Schwarze, die oft für eine Weiße gehalten wird, hat sich Piper in mehreren ihrer Arbeiten—darunter *My Call(ing) Card #1* und das "bekenntnishafte" *Political Self-Portrait # 2*—mit der einzigartigen Situation des rassischen Dazwischenstehens beschäftigt. Das Video—in einer Ecke installiert und durch einen umgedrehten Tisch verbarrikadiert—besteht aus einem anscheinend aufrichtigen und unschuldigen Monolog Pipers. An den Wänden hinter dem Monitor sind zwei Geburtsurkunden von Pipers Vater angebracht, eine gibt seine Rasse als weiß, die andere als schwarz an. Zurechtgemacht, wie sie selbst sagt, als "bürgerlich-adrette junge Miss" gibt sie gleich zu Beginn bekannt: "Ich bin eine Schwarze". Worauf dann die Aufforderung folgt, "Nun setzen wir uns einmal gemeinsam mit dieser sozialen Tatsache und der Tatsache, daß ich es ausspreche, auseinander". In den folgenden 16 Minuten erörtert Piper die verschiedenen möglichen Reaktionen des

Fig. 14
Adrian Piper
Cornered, 1988
installation view
Cat. no. 13

In this respect, Adrian Piper's videotape/installation *Cornered* (fig. 14) is an especially important work, provoking unacknowledged or unrecognized racism even as it performs an elegant deconstruction of the American cultural *mythos* of whiteness and blackness. A light-skinned black woman, often taken for white, Piper has addressed in several of her works—including *My Calling (Card) #1* and the "confessional" *Political Self-portrait #2*—the singular state of racial in-betweenness. Installed in a corner, and barricaded by an up-ended table, the video consists of an ostensibly straightforward monologue by Piper. On the walls behind the monitor are mounted two birth certificates of Piper's father, one giving his race as white, the other as black. Dressed and coiffed, as she describes it, in "bourgie, junior-miss style," she begins with the announcement, "I'm black," followed by the injunction, "Now, let's deal with this social fact, and the fact of my stating it, together." In the next 16 minutes, Piper proceeds to interrogate the various possible responses of the presumed white viewer to her statement, parsing out the racist implications of the viewer's reactions. About midway through the monologue, Piper reports that "some researchers have estimated that almost all purportedly white Americans have between 5% and 20% black ancestry" and thus, according to entrenched racial conventions, are to be considered as black. The possible reactions to this information are then themselves pursued, culminating with the injunction that this shared black identity is not just Piper's, but "our problem to solve...Now how do you propose we solve it? What are you going to do?" The tape closes with white letters on a black ground—"Welcome to the struggle."

Although the word "miscegenation" is never uttered, one of the complex themes within the work is the

angenommenen weißen Zuschauers auf ihre Erklärung und arbeitet deren rassistische Implikationen heraus. Etwa in der Mitte ihres Monologs berichtet sie, daß "nach Schätzung einiger Wissenschaftler fast alle vorgeblich weißen Amerikaner zwischen 5 und 20 Prozent schwarzes Blut haben", somit also—nach den gängigen rassischen Konventionen—als schwarz zu betrachten wären. Die möglichen Reaktionen auf diese Information werden nun ihrerseits weiterverfolgt und gipfeln schließlich in der Feststellung, daß diese gemeinsame schwarze Identität nicht nur das Problem Pipers sei, sondern "das Problem, das wir alle lösen müssen ... Also, was meinen *Sie*, wie wir es lösen sollen? Was werden *Sie* tun?" Das Video endet mit weißen Buchstaben auf schwarzem Grund—"Welcome to the Struggle".

Obwohl das Wort "Rassenmischung" nie fällt, ist eines der komplexen Themen der Arbeit die verdrängte Geschichte sexueller Beziehungen zwischen den Rassen in Amerika, eine Geschichte, die selbst das Erbe der Sklaverei und ihrer zahllosen Greuel ist. Auch das wirft die Frage nach der Natur und den Bedingungen von Identität auf, denn, wie Judith Wilson in ihrer Erörterung von *Political Self-Portrait #2* aufzeigt:

> ...während die äußere Erscheinung in der täglichen Praxis meist das einzige Kriterium der Rassenfeststellung ist, definieren Recht und Gesetz der U.S.A. Rasse als Produkt der Abstammung—ein äußerst unverläßlicher Indikator physischer Merkmale wie jeder, der sich an Mendels "Gesetz der unabhängigen Verteilung" erinnert, schnell begreifen wird. Philosophisch gesprochen ist das Problem mit der Bildung von Bewußtsein verbunden. Wenn Identität sozial konstituiert wird und auf die Assimilation von in den Augen anderer gespiegelten Selbstbildern hinausläuft und wenn Rasse in der Praxis aufgrund des Aussehens, dem Prinzip nach aber aufgrund der Abstammung bestimmt wird, was konstituiert dann die "rassische Identität" von Personen, deren Aussehen nicht mit ihrer angeblichen Abstammung übereinstimmt?[21]

repressed history of interracial sexual relations in American history, a history that is itself the legacy of slavery and its myriad violences. This too poses a question about the nature and terms of identity, for as Judith Wilson points out in her discussion of *Political Self-portrait #2*:

> ...while physical appearance is frequently the sole criterion for determining race in daily practice, U.S. law and custom define race as the product of genealogy—a highly variable predicator of physical traits as anyone who recalls Mendel's "law of independent assortment" will readily grasp. In philosophical terms, the problem relates to the operation of consciousness. If identity is socially constructed and amounts to the assimilation of images of self reflected in the eyes of others, and if race is determined in practice by appearance and in principle by ancestry, what constitutes the "racial identity" of individuals whose appearance is at odds with their alleged ancestry?[21]

This discursive instability at the heart of racial identity runs counter to assumptions underlying other discursive constructions of identity that posit its fixed and irreducible essence. In this regard, it is especially suggestive that recent writing on the subject by theorists such as Hortense Spillers focuses on the kind of "in-betweenness" that Piper explores in certain of her works. For example, in an extraordinary essay on the mulatta/o, Spillers elaborates what she terms the "neither/nor" status of a female subject whose very coloration, as well as its origin, disrupts the categorical distinctions upon which racial divisions are predicated:

> Created to provide a middle ground of latitude between "black" and "white," mulatto being a neither/nor proposition—inscribed in no historic locus or materiality—could therefore be only evasive and shadowy on the national landscape. To that extent, the mulatto/a embodied an alibi, an excuse for "other/otherness" that the dominant culture could not (cannot now either) appropriate or wish away... Behind the African-become-American stands the shadow, the insubstantial "double" that the culture dreamed *in the place of* that humanity transformed into its profoundest challenge and by the impositions of policy, its deepest "un-American" activity.[22]

Such explorations of the "neither/nors" of racial, sexual, and cultural identities not only foster more complex, more nuanced perceptions of the multiple determinations of identity, but open up more fluid and supple political deployments of them. This is particularly evident in the range of theoretical and cultural production concerned with the notion of "borderlands" identities, that is to say, identities which, like Spillers' neither/nor, are constituted precisely by the *imbrication* of the cultures of dominant

Diese diskursive Instabilität im Zentrum der rassischen Identität durchkreuzt Annahmen anderer diskursiver Konstruktionen von Identität, die von einer feststehenden, unveränderlichen Essenz ausgehen. In diesem Zusammenhang ist es besonders aufschlußreich, daß sich auch neuere theoretische Schriften zum Thema von Leuten wie Hortense Spillers beispielsweise auf dieses "Dazwischenstehen" konzentrieren, das Piper in gewissen Arbeiten auslotet. In einem außerordentlichen Essay über die Mulattin/den Mulatten entwickelt Spillers das, was sie als "weder/noch"-Status eines weiblichen Subjekts bezeichnet, das sowohl durch seine Färbung als auch durch seine Abstammung die Kategorien, auf denen Rassenunterscheidungen beruhen, erschüttert:

> Erfunden als Zwischenbereich zwischen "Schwarz" und "Weiß" konnte der Mulatte—als Weder/Noch-Begriff, der an keinem historischen Ort und in keiner historischen Materialität festgeschrieben war—nur eine ungreifbare und schemenhafte Figur in der historischen Landschaft sein. Insofern verkörperte der Mulatte/die Mulattin ein Alibi, einen Vorwand für das "Andere", das sich die herrschende Kultur weder aneignen noch fortwünschen konnte (und auch heute nicht kann) ... Hinter dem zum Amerikaner gewordenen Afrikaner steht der Schatten, das immaterielle "Double", das sich die Kultur anstelle dieses Menschen erträumt hat, der zu ihrer größten Herausforderung und—durch die Einwirkungen der Politik—zu ihrer fundamentalsten "unamerikanischen Aktivität" wurde.[22]

Solche Erkundungen des "Weder/Noch" rassischer, geschlechtlicher und kultureller Identitäten fördern nicht nur komplexere, differenziertere Wahrnehmungsweisen der vielfältigen Determinanten von Identität, sondern eröffnen auch flexiblere politische Einsatzmöglichkeiten derselben. Dies wird besonders deutlich in der Fülle der theoretischen und kulturellen Produktionen, die sich mit "Grenz"-Identitäten beschäftigen, mit Identitäten also, die wie Spillers' "Weder/Noch" aus der *Verflechtung* der dominanten und der subalternen Kultur, der Kultur der Beherrscher und der der Beherrschten entstehen. Auch das ist eine Alchimie individueller wie kultureller Identität, ein Synkretismus, der die hybriden Bewußtseins- und Identitätsformen hervorbringt, die nicht nur prägende Elemente der sozialen Wirklichkeit in den Vereinigten Staaten sind, sondern auch *das* Kennzeichen der Postmoderne.

Guillermo Gómez-Peña, dessen *Border Brujo* ["Der Schamane"] (Fig. 15) in der Video-Sektion der Ausstellung zu sehen ist, ist sowohl als Künstler wie auch als prägnanter Kulturtheoretiker mit dem Bereich der Grenzkultur und Grenzidentität verbunden. Die Kunst des gebürtigen Mexikaners, der seit 1978 in den USA lebt, ist—wie die Pipers—dem Erbe des Konzeptualismus verpflichtet und umfaßt—auch darin

Fig. 15
Guillermo Gómez-Peña
video still from *Border Brujo* [Shaman], 1990
Cat. no. 28

and subaltern, oppressor and oppressed. This too is an alchemy of both individual and cultural identity, a syncretism that produces the hybridized forms of consciousness and identity that are both shaping elements of social formation in the U.S. and the very hallmark of postmodernity.

Guillermo Gómez-Peña, whose *Border Brujo* [Shaman] (fig. 15) is included in the video portion of the exhibition, is associated both as an artist and as an incisive cultural theorist with the implications of borderlands culture and identity. Mexican-born, and a resident of the U.S. since 1978, Gómez-Peña's art, like Piper's, is grounded in the legacy of conceptualism and, also like hers, embraces a wide range of forms—book art, poetry, and film, but perhaps most influentially, performance art (*Border Brujo* is actually a video version of a performance). In a recent statement in *Art in America*, Gómez-Peña sketched some of the conditions and possibilities of hybridization, noting in passing that in the U.S., the art world and the educational system are the major battlegrounds in the multiculturalism debate:

> In the last 25 years [Third World] immigrants have changed the West, almost to the point where the West is no longer the West. Asia and Latin America live in the U.S. in the same way that North Africa lives in Europe. A storm has shattered all racial, economic and cultural parameters. The U.S. is no longer the heir of

derjenigen Pipers ähnlich—eine breite Palette von Ausdrucksformen—Buchkunst, Gedichte, Film und—vielleicht am einflußreichsten—Performance (auch *Border Brujo* ist eigentlich die Video-Fassung einer Performance). In einem Artikel in *Art in America* hat Gómez-Peña kürzlich einige der Bedingungen und Möglichkeiten der Hybridation skizziert, wobei er anmerkte, daß die Hauptschauplätze der Multikulturalismus-Debatte in den USA die Kunstwelt und das Bildungssystem seien:

> In den letzten 25 Jahren haben [Einwanderer aus der dritten Welt] den Westen verändert—fast so sehr, daß es nicht mehr der Westen ist. Asien und Lateinamerika leben in den USA so, wie Nordafrika in Europa lebt. Ein Sturm hat sämtliche rassischen, ökonomischen und kulturellen Parameter in Trümmer gelegt. Die USA sind nicht länger die Erben der westlichen, europäischen Kultur. Stattdessen sind sie ein bizarres Laboratorium, in dem alle Rassen und Kontinente mit ihrer Identität experimentieren in dem Versuch, ein neues Modell des Zusammenlebens zu finden. In diesem Prozeß entstehen ungeheuer aufregende hybride Identitäten und hybride Kunstformen. Leider entstehen auch Gewalt, Mißverständnis und Angst.
> Sprechen wir über drei Quellen kultureller Identität. Die eine ist von oben durch den Staat diktierte. Diese Art der Identität ist im allgemeinen fiktiv und gehorcht den Plänen der Regierungen, die sie erzwingen. Dann gibt es eine Identität, die von unten kommt, aus den Traditionen und Erinnerungen bestimmter Gruppen einer Gesellschaft. Diese Identität gerät häufig in Konflikt mit der von oben. Direkt aus der Gemeinschaft heraus entstehend ist sie wesentlich beweglicher und in ständiger Veränderung, da sie für Fusionen und kulturelle Koalitionen offen ist. Ich möchte aber noch ein drittes Modell vorschlagen: das hybrider Zwischenidentitäten oder multipler zusammengesetzter Identitäten... Diese neuen [Identitäts-] Modelle, die ich als Hybride bezeichne, sind das, was mich eigentlich interessiert; sie sprechen für die Zukunft dieses Landes und des ganzen Kontinents. Die heutige Chicano-Kultur, die afroamerikanische oder asiatoamerikanische Kultur sind offene Systeme im ständigen Wandel.[23]

Border Brujo ist eine Art Ein-Mann-Theater der Grenzkultur und Grenzidentität, in dem Gómez-Peña eine Vielzahl verschiedener Rollen annimmt, sich durch kulturelle Codes, Zeichen, Sprachen und Identitäten schlägt und so den Gemeinplatz verkörpert, daß die "Grenze" trotz all ihrer Manifestationen ein Bewußtseinszustand ist. Hinter einem altarähnlichen Tisch—beladen unter anderem mit reliösen Paraphernalien—versetzt sich Gómez-Peña in die Rollen eines Ersatz-Schamanen, eines urbanen Cholo-Punks, eines illegalen mexikanischen Einwanderers, eines Gringo, eines Banditen usw. und tischt dabei ein komplettes Menü an Sprachen, Dialekten, Jargons auf. Manchmal ist die Sprache selbst Nonsense weder dem Englisch- noch dem Spanischsprecher verständlich. Die sprachliche Verunsicherung beider Zuschauergruppen scheint ein integraler Bestandteil von Gómez-Peñas künstlerischer

Western European culture. Instead, it is a bizarre laboratory in which all races and all continents are experimenting with identity, trying to find a new model of conviviality. In this process, very exciting kinds of hybrid identities and hybrid art forms are being created. Unfortunately, violence, misunderstanding and fear are also created.

Let us talk about three sources of cultural identity. One is imposed from above by the state. This kind of identity, generally speaking, is fictitious and responds to the agendas of the governments that enforce it. Then there is an identity which comes from below, from the traditions and memories of specific groups within a society. This identity often enters into conflict with the one from above. Generated at the grass-roots level, it is much more fluid and, because it is open to fusion and cultural negotiation, it is constantly changing. I would also propose a third model: that of hybrid and transitional identities, of multiple and hyphenated identities...These new models [of identity], which I call hybrids, are what truly interest me; they speak for the future of this country and the entire continent. Contemporary Chicano, African-American or Asian-American cultures are dynamic, open systems in constant transformation.[23]

Border Brujo is a kind of one-man theater of borderlands culture and identity in which Gómez-Peña assumes a variety of roles, scrambling cultural codes, signifiers, languages, and identities, enacting the truism that the "border" is, for all its diverse manifestations, a state of mind. Behind an altar-like table, laden, among other things, with religious paraphernalia, Gómez-Peña, variously inhabits the roles of ersatz shaman, urban cholo-punk, wetback, gringo, bandito, and so forth, deploying a full menu of languages, dialects, argots. Occasionally, his language is itself a non-sense, comprehensible neither to Anglophone nor Spanish speakers. The linguistic mystification of both types of spectators appears to be an integral part of Gómez-Peña's artistic strategy, suggesting that no single language adequately encompasses, mirrors, or translates the protean and variegated elements that make up the borderlands. In Gómez-Peña's work, this concept of borderlands is by no means a discrete entity. More precisely, it is both a process and a condition, akin to what is called "the postmodern condition." Neither euphoric nor dysphoric, Gómez-Peña's borderlands represents a cultural conjunction productive of new subjectivities and identities, a diagnostic that exceeds in its precision the often wooly notion of multiculturalism. It is, moreover, a formulation that explicitly acknowledges differences within:

> United States Latino culture is not homogeneous. It includes a multiplicity of artistic and intellectual expressions both rural and urban, traditional and experimental, marginal and dominant. These expres-

Strategie zu sein und deutet darauf hin, daß die proteischen, vielgestaltigen Elemente des Grenzlands durch keine einzelne Sprache adäquat erfaßt, wiedergegeben oder übersetzt werden können. In Gómez-Peñas Arbeiten ist dieses Konzept des Grenzlands keineswegs eine klar abgegrenzte Einheit. Oder—besser gesagt—es ist gleichzeitig ein Prozeß und ein Zustand und gleicht damit dem, was als "condition postmoderne" bezeichnet wurde. Weder euphorisch noch dysphorisch repräsentieren Gómez-Peñas Grenzlande einen kulturellen Zusammenprall, der neue Subjektivitäten und Identitäten entstehen läßt, eine Diagnose, die in ihrer Präzision über die oft vage Idee des Multikulturalismus hinausgeht. Es ist überdies auch eine Form, die innere Differenzen ausdrücklich anerkennt:

> Die Latinokultur in den USA ist nicht homogen. Sie umfaßt eine ganze Reihe verschiedener künstlerischer und intellektueller Ausdrucksformen, ländlicher wie urbaner, traditioneller wie experimenteller, marginaler wie dominanter. Diese Ausdrucksformen unterscheiden sich voneinander je nach Klasse, Geschlecht, Nationalität, Ideologie, Landschaft, politischem Kontext, Grad der Marginalität oder Assimilation und Dauer des Aufenthalts in den USA.
>
> Kalifornische Chicanos und New Yorker Puertorikaner leben in unterschiedlichen Kulturlandschaften. Selbst innerhalb der Chicano-Kultur hat ein Dichter aus einer ländlichen Gemeinde in New Mexico sehr wenig gemein mit einem urbanen Cholo-Punk aus L.A. Die rechtsgerichteten Kubaner aus Miami sind bedingungslose Gegner der linken südamerikanischen Exilanten. Die kulturellen Ausdrucksweisen zentralamerikanischer oder mexikanischer Gastarbeiter unterscheiden sich drastisch von der Latino-Intelligenzia an den Universitäten usw. ad infinitum.[24]

In Anbetracht der kulturellen Tatsache der inneren Unterschiedlichkeit des Grenzlandes—auch was seine divergenten und oft gegensätzlichen politischen Ausformungen betrifft—ist jede einheitliche oder selbst vereinte Identitätspolitik ganz offensichtlich von vornherein ausgeschlossen. Dennoch hat die diskursive Neuskizzierung der Landkarte der amerikanischen Kultur, mit der sich Gómez-Peñas künstlerische Aktivitäten im weitesten Sinn umreißen lassen, starke politische Implikationen. In erster Linie weil sie versucht, den phantasmatischen Glauben an ein weißes, angelsächsisches Amerika zu erschüttern, das sich als verschieden und losgelöst von jenen "anderen" begreift, deren Mitvorhandensein eigentlich nur eine logische Folge der amerikanischen Geschichte ist. Andererseits korrigiert sie aber auch den ebenso phantasmatischen Glauben, daß sich subalterne Kulturen eine zeitlose und ahistorische Reinheit oder Essenz bewahren könnten. Womit vielmehr gearbeitet werden muß, was tatsächlich *er*arbeitet werden muß, ist die viel schwierigere Akzeptanz der

sions differ from one another according to class, sex, nationality, ideology, geography, political context, degree of marginality or assimilation, and time spent in the U.S. California Chicanos and Nuyoricans inhabit different cultural landscapes. Even within Chicano culture a poet living in a rural community in New Mexico has very little in common with an urban cholo-punk from L.A. Right wing Cubanos from Miami are unconditional adversaries of leftist South American exiles. The cultural expressions of Central American and Mexican migrant workers differ drastically from those of the Latino intelligentsia in the universities, *ad infinitum*.[24]

Confronting the cultural fact of borderlands diversity, including its divergent and often opposed internal political formulations, must obviously preclude any notion of a unitary, or even unified, identity politics. Nevertheless, the kind of discursive remapping of American culture that in the broadest sense describes Gómez-Peña's artistic activity has potent political implications. Most importantly, it seeks to dissolve the fantasmatic belief in a white, Anglo-Saxon America distinct and apart from those "others" whose very co-presence is in fact the consequence of America's own history. Conversely, it corrects the equally fantasmatic belief that subaltern cultures can preserve an atemporal and ahistorical purity or essence. What is to be worked with, what indeed remains to be worked *through*, is the far more difficult acceptance of multiplicity, diversity, and difference itself.

Gómez-Peña's notion of a borderlands identity, an identity that by definition is plural, "impure," and in constant flux has certain correspondences with the no less hybridized art of Jimmie Durham, a Cherokee. Durham, like Piper and Gómez-Peña, works in a broad range of media (installation, performance, assemblage and carving, image/text works, poetry and critical writing). In much of Durham's art, the model of identity appears most closely to approximate Claude Levi-Strauss' concept of bricolage, whereby cultural identity, far from being a holistic, "authentic," and integral given, is rather a syncretic, piecemeal, and aggregate affair, cobbled together from disparate, random, even antithetical elements. Formulated with respect to ostensibly traditional and "tribal" cultures (and thus an explicit critique of Western romantic notions of authentic cultural or ethnic identity—products themselves of the Western imaginary), the concept has nonetheless a descriptive relevance in other contexts.

In Durham's work, the political context is, of course, the morass of contradiction, historical crime and

Vielgestaltigkeit, Verschiedenartigkeit und Differenz selbst.

Gómez-Peñas Konzept einer Grenzlandidentität, einer Identität, die per definitionem plural, "unrein" und ständig in Fluß ist, weist gewisse Parallelen mit der nicht weniger hybriden Kunst von Jimmie Durham auf, einem Cherokesen. Durham arbeitet wie Piper und Gómez-Peña in einer Vielzahl von Medien (Installation, Performance, Bildhauerei und Schnitzerei, Bild/Text-Arbeiten, Gedichte und kritische Schriften). Sein Identitätsmodell scheint in vielen seiner Arbeiten am ehesten Claude Levi-Strauss' Idee der Bricolage zu entsprechen, wonach kulturelle Identität keineswegs eine holistische, "authentische", gegebene Ganzheit ist, sondern ein synkretistisches, aggregiertes Stückwerk, zusammengestoppelt aus disparaten, zufälligen und selbst gegensätzlichen Elementen. Entwickelt im Hinblick auf vermeintlich traditionelle "Stammes"-Kulturen (und damit eine ausdrückliche Kritik romantischer Vorstellungen von authentischer kultureller oder ethnischer Identität—Ausgeburten westlicher Imagination) ist dieses Konzept jedoch auch in anderen Kontexten von deskriptivem Wert.

In Durhams Werk besteht der politische Kontext natürlich in dem Morast aus Widersprüchen, historischen Verbrechen und ihrer Verleugnung, mächtigen kulturellen Mythologien, Enteignung und Verelendung, welche zusammengenommen die Lebensbedingungen der amerikanischen Urbevölkerung in den heutigen USA ausmachen. Sich selbst zum "universalen Cherokesen-Künstler" stilisierend und seine Arbeit als eine Mischung aus "Neo-Primitivismus und Neo-Konzeptualismus" charakterisierend durchbrechen Durhams Person *wie* seine Kunst jedoch genau die Begriffe und Definitionen, deren sich diese Charakterisierungen bedienen. So demontiert die Bezeichnung "universaler Cherokesen-Künstler" zum Beispiel sehr wirksam den Imperialismus, der dem Anspruch auf Universalität (historisch dem weißen männlichen Subjekt zugeschrieben) zugrundeliegt, während die paradoxe Charakterisierung "Neo-Primitivismus und Neo-Konzeptualismus" auf ein Unterlaufen kunsthistorischer und stilistischer Kategorien verweist, eine "Bricolage" nominell antithetischer künstlerischer Praktiken.[25]

Die Theorie der Bricolage trifft aber nicht nur auf die in Durhams Werk evozierten gegenwärtigen Realitäten der Identität der amerikanischen Urbevölkerung zu, sondern auch auf seine Arbeitsweise. *Bedia's Stirring Wheel* (Fig. 16) ist ein gutes Beispiel. Es ist eine etwa 1,20 m hohe freistehende Skulptur, deren "Skelett" aus einem Autolenkrad mit Lenksäule besteht, die in einer Radfelge verankert ist. Umwickelt mit Tierhäuten und Fellen und verziert mit einem Stoff

Fig. 16
Jimmie Durham
Bedia's Stirring Wheel, 1985
Cat. no. 1

its disavowal, potent cultural mythologies, expropriation and immiseration that collectively constitute the circumstances of Native American peoples in the contemporary U.S. Its artistic context is no less fraught. Fashioning himself "a universal Cherokee artist" and characterizing his art as a mix of "neo-primitivism and neo-conceptualism," Durham's persona *and* his art disrupt the very terms and definitions these characterizations would denote. Thus, while the designation "universal Cherokee artist" effectively dismantles the imperialism that underpins pretensions to universality (historically attributed to a white male subject), the oxymoronic "neo-primitivism and neo-conceptualism" signals a subversion of art historical and stylistic categories, a "bricolage" of nomimally antithetical art practices.[25]

The theory of bricolage applies not only to the contemporary realities of Native-American identity as they are evoked in Durham's work, but to his way of working as well. *Bedia's Stirring Wheel* (fig. 16) is a case in point. A free-standing floor piece, approximately four feet high, its "skeleton" consists of an automobile steering wheel and column embedded in a wheel rim. Wrapped with animal hides, skins, and fur, embellished with star-printed fabric, beaded belts, tassels, animal tail (suspended from the gear shift), cartoon-figure button, and various other elements both natural and synthetic, *Bedia's Stirring Wheel* occupies some middle ground between ritual object and souvenir stand. Its accompanying text, however, is integral to the work:

Bedia's Stirring Wheel
From: Site B, Quadrant 71, White Planes, New York

> José Bedia, the famous Cuban explorer/archeologist, discovered this stirring wheel, sometimes referred to as the "Fifth" or "Big" wheel, during the second excavation of the ruins of White Planes in 3290 A.D. He believes that the stirring wheel was a symbol of office for the Great White Father, often called, "the Man Behind the Wheel." Bedia claims that the chief would stand behind the wheel to make pronouncements and stirring speeches.

Playful and punning, the description of the *Stirring Wheel* apes the form and content of the labels typically encountered in anthropological, ethnographic, or natural history museums. Reading the signs of our vanished civilization, interpreting our enigmatic artifacts, the excavators, as we might have predicted, get things wrong as, by implication, do all the institutions that profess to represent the cultures they embalm. That José Bedia, a contemporary Cuban artist and friend of Durham, has the last word on the

mit Sternmuster, mit glasperlenbesetzen Gürteln, mit Quasten, einem Tierschwanz (der an der Gangschaltung hängt), einem Comic-Figur-Button und diversen anderen natürlichen wie synthetischen Elementen ist *Bedia's Stirring Wheel* ein Mittelding zwischen Ritualobjekt und Souvenierstand. Dazu kommt als integraler Bestandteil der Arbeit der Begleittext:

Bedia's Stirring Wheel (Feuerrad)
Fundstelle B, Quadrant 71, White Planes, New York

> José Bedia, der berühmte kubanische Forscher/Archäologe, entdeckte dieses Feuerrad—gelegentlich auch als "fünftes" oder "großes" Rad bezeichnet—bei der zweiten Ausgrabung der Ruinen von White Plains im Jahre 3290 A.D. Er vermutet, daß das Feuerrad ein Amtssymbol des großen weißen Vaters war, der häufig auch der "Mann am Feuer" genannt wurde. Von diesem Rad aus, so behauptet Bedia, hat der Häuptling seine Verlautbarungen gemacht und seine anfeuernden Reden gehalten.

Die wortspielerische Beschreibung des *Stirring Wheel* (eigentl.: Umrühr-, Aufwühlrad, was zusätzlich auf die Tätigkeit des Archäologen wie auch des Künstlers verweist, ein Aspekt der in der deutschen Widergabe des Wortspiels verlorengeht—*Anm. d. Übers.*) imitiert in Form und Inhalt die typischen Etikettierungen, denen man in anthropologischen, ethnographischen oder naturkundlichen Museen begegnet. Bei ihrer Deutung der Zeichen unserer verschwundenen Kultur, ihrer Interpretation unserer rätselhaften Artefakte bringen die Archäologen, wie vorhersehbar, einiges durcheinander—genauso wie all die Institutionen, die sich anmaßen, die Kulturen zu repräsentieren, die sie konservieren. Daß José Bedia, ein zeitgenössischer kubanischer Künstler und Freund Durhams, das letzte Wort über die Bedeutung des Kunstwerks hat, ist nicht ohne eigenes politisches Gewicht.

Aber wie schon angedeutet, hat der bricolageartige Aufbau von *Bedia's Stirring Wheel* weiterreichende Implikationen. Durhams Auffassung von der Identität der amerikanischen Ureinwohner im heutigen Amerika—einschließlich seiner eigenen—bekennt sich zur Unmöglichkeit einer Rückkehr zu einem einstigen Zustand der kulturellen Gnade. Tatsächlich gehört es zum bitteren Vermächtnis des Schicksals der amerikanischen Ureinwohner, zwischen einer unwiederbringlichen Vergangenheit und einer für viele freud- und ausweglosen Gegenwart zu stehen. Dies ist der Un-Ort der Enterbten: "Einer der schrecklichsten Aspekte unserer heutigen Situation ist, daß sich niemand von uns als richtiger Indianer fühlt... Zum Großteil fühlen wir uns schuldig und versuchen, dem Bild zu entsprechen, das der weiße Mann von uns zeichnet."[26]

Die Bricolage ist daher sowohl ein deskriptives Modell der Identität wie auch eine Strategie, ihr einen Sinn zu

Fig. 17
Theresa Hak Kyung Cha
video still from *Exileé*, 1978
Cat. no. 27

meaning of the artifact is not without its own political
import.

But as I have indicated, the bricolage-like
construction of *Bedia's Stirring Wheel* possesses wider
implications. Durham's notion of Native-American identity in contemporary America—including his own—
acknowledges the impossibility of a return to a prior state
of cultural grace. Indeed, it is part of the bitter legacy
of the Native-American experience to be suspended
between an irrecoverable past and, for many, a bleak and
thwarted present. This is the non-place of the disinher-
ited: "One of the most terrible aspects of our situation
today is that none of us feel that we are real Indians...For
the most part we feel guilty and try to measure up to the
white man's definition of ourselves."[26]

Accordingly, bricolage is both a descriptive
model of identity and a strategy for making some kind
of sense of it. One works, after all, with what one has,
both physically and aesthetically. The protean elements
with which Durham constructs his objects—including
the discarded flotsam and jetsam, the cast-offs of contemporary society—can be thought of as a defiant act of
salvage, reconstituting an identity, however provisional,
from the wreckage of genocide and racism.

Like the condition of blacks in white America,
that of Native Americans needs to be considered *sui
generis*. Similarly, the circumstances and determinations
by which Asian-American identities are constituted must
be considered not merely under the generic rubric of
"immigration" (whether economically or politically
motivated), but with respect to the singularity of the

geben. Man arbeitet schließlich mit dem, was man hat, sowohl
körperlich als auch ästhetisch. Die proteischen Elemente, aus
denen Durham seine Objekte baut—einschließlich des ausran-
gierten Trödelkrams, des Abfalls der heutigen Gesellschaft—
deuten auf einen trotzigen Akt der Rettung, der Wiederherstel-
lung einer—wie immer provisorischen—Identität aus den
Überresten von Völkermord und Rassismus.

Wie die Situation der Schwarzen im weißen Amerika
muß auch die der amerikanischen Ureinwohner *sui generis*
betrachtet werden. Ähnlich dürfen auch die Umstände und
Bedingungen, durch die asiatoamerikanische Identitäten
geprägt werden, nicht nur unter der Rubrik "Einwanderung"
(ob aus ökonomischen oder politischen Gründen) betrachtet
werden, sondern müssen mit Blick auf die Besonderheiten der
Mutterkultur in deren Überschneidung mit den Erfahrungen
des Einwanderers in Amerika gesehen werden.

Offiziell sind Yong Soon Min und die verstorbene
Theresa Hak Kyung Cha Koreoamerikanerinnen, aber im
Falle beider Künstlerinnen gibt es noch die feiner unterschei-
dende Etikettierung "Halb-Koreoamerikanerin", womit eine
Person gemeint ist, die in Korea geboren, aber in den USA
aufgewachsen ist (also weder voll als amerikanisch noch voll
als koreanisch betrachtet wird—ein weiteres "Weder/Noch"
im Kalkül ethnischer und kultureller Identität).

Cha, die 1982 im Alter von 31 Jahren in New York
City ermordet wurde, hat ein gehalt- und beziehungsreiches
Werk hinterlassen bestehend aus Videos, Buchkunst, Collagen
und Assemblagen, nebst einer Anthologie von filmtheoreti-
schen Texten.[27] (Ihre Performances wurden unglücklicher-
weise nicht dokumentiert). Die theoretische Ausgeklügeltheit
und Komplexität von Chas Werk, die sie in all diesen Medien
demonstriert, ist nicht weniger frappierend als seine sparsame,
poetische Schönheit. Bei ihr verband sich eine äußerst feine
ästhetische Sensibilität mit einer rigorosen spekulativen Intelli-
genz, die auf eine breite Palette von Disziplinen zurückgriff—
Filmtheorie, Linguistik, Semiotik und Psychoanalyse. Obwohl
der Form nach proteisch, war Chas Werk in seinen Fragestellungen durchaus konsistent. Diese kreisten vor allem um das
Problem der Dislozierung—der geographischen, der kulturellen, der sprachlichen und der historischen. Vor allen Dingen
war es aber die Sprache, die ihr als zentraler Tropus für die
Wunden des Exils diente. Sie charakterisierte ihre Arbeit
einmal als "Suche nach den Wurzeln der Sprache, ehe sie
auf der Zungenspitze zur Welt kommt". Dieses temporale
"ehe" ist entscheidend: es zeigt, daß Cha nicht nur von der
Materialität der Sprache (Koreanisch, Englisch, Französisch)
in ihrer mündlichen, schriftlichen und bildlichen Dimension

Fig. 18a
Yong Soon Min
deCOLONIZATION, 1991
detail
Cat. no. 11

parent culture as it intersects with the immigrants' experience of America.

The official designation of Yong Soon Min and the late Theresa Hak Kyung Cha is Korean American. Yet in both artists' cases, the appellation is further distinguished as "1.5 generation Korean American," meaning someone born in Korea but brought up in the U.S. (not first-generation American, but not considered fully Korean—another "neither/nor" in the calculus of ethnic and cultural identity).

Murdered in New York City in 1982 at the age of 31, Cha left behind her a rich and allusive body of work, including videotapes, book art, collage, and assemblage in addition to an anthology of film theory.[27] (Her performance work, unfortunately, was not documented.) The theoretical sophistication and complexity of Cha's work, demonstrated throughout these media, is no less striking than its austere and poetic beauty. A highly refined aesthetic sensibility was joined to a rigorous and speculative intelligence that drew from an equally wide range of disciplines—film theory, linguistics, semiotics, and psychoanalysis. Although protean in form, Cha's work is quite consistent in its preoccupations, which center on issues of displacement—geographic, cultural, linguistic, historic. Of these it was preeminently language that functioned as the master trope for the wounds of exile. In one artist's statement, she characterized her work as "looking for the roots of language before it is born on the tip of the tongue." This temporal "before" is

fasziniert war, sondern auch von deren flüchtigen und evokativen Eigenschaften, ihrer Verbindung mit dem Gedächtnis, mit der Subjektivität und mit dem Unbewußten. Und obwohl die eigentliche Quelle ihres Werks direkt aus der Erfahrung der Immigration und des Exils kommt—dem Verlust der Muttersprache und dem Trauma der Entwurzelung—läßt es sich auch als ein Werk sehen, das vor allem die Schwierigkeit zeigt, eine "Sprache" zu finden, in der man "anders" sprechen kann. Eine solche Sprache wäre eine Form der künstlerischen Rede, die einerseits den Signifikanten aus seinen Fesseln befreit, sein freies Flottieren ermöglicht, andererseits aber auch eine Art Vereinigung mit dem Zuschauer anstrebt, eine gemeinschaftliche Sinnproduktion. Dies muß man im Zusammenhang mit feministischen Versuchen einer Umgestaltung und Veränderung von Ausdrucksformen sehen—vor allem der Sprache— die von den symbolischen Strukturen und der Logik des Patriarchats bestimmt sind.

In der Videoarbeit *Exilée* (Fig. 17) aus dem Jahr 1980, zu der ursprünglich auch ein Film gehörte, der auf die Wand projiziert wurde, in die der Monitor eingelassen war, erkundet Cha sowohl die wirkliche, bei der Bewegung von einem Ort zum anderen verflossene Zeit (von Korea nach Amerika, 10 Stunden 23 Minuten) als auch deren mehr abstrakte und internalisierte Manifestationen. Standbilder von Wolken—aufgenommen aus einem Flugzeug—rufen eine zusätzliche Empfindung räumlicher und zeitlicher Bewegung hervor, während Chas Stimme traurig die verschiedenen Verluste des Exils intoniert: "kein name/außer dem gegebenen/letzter...abwesender...name/ohne namen/ein nullname/

Fig. 18b
Yong Soon Min
deCOLONIZATION, 1991
installation view
Cat. no. 11

important: it signals Cha's fascination not only with the materiality of language (Korean, English, or French) in its aural, written, and visual dimensions, but also with its elusive and evocative properties, its links to memory, subjectivity, and the unconscious. And while the well-springs of Cha's work are related directly to the experience of immigration and exile—the loss of the mother tongue and the trauma of displacement—her work can nonetheless be seen to foreground the difficulty of finding a "language" in which to speak "otherly." Such a language would be a form of artistic speech that both unshackles the signifier—allows for its free play—yet promotes a form of communion with the spectator, a collaborative production of meaning. This needs to be understood in the context of feminist attempts to remodel and transform those aspects of expression—particularly language—marked by the symbolic structures and logic of patriarchy.

In the 1980 tape *Exilée* (fig. 17), which in its original form included a film projected upon a screen wall within which the video monitor was placed, Cha explores both the literal, elapsed time of movement from one place to the other (Korea to America, ten hours and 23 minutes) as well as its more abstract and internalized manifestations. Still images of clouds seen from a plane further evoke the sensation of spatial and temporal passage, while Cha's voice mournfully intones the various losses of exile: "no name/none other than given/last...absent...name/without name/a no name/between name." In this, as in other works, a linkage is implied between the difficulties of cultural and linguistic displacement and the problematic relations of women to speech and identity.

Yong Soon Min is almost an exact contemporary of Cha's, and in fact the two were friends at Berkeley, where both were students in the 1970s. As Min has described her own artistic trajectory, engaging issues of identity as a subject for her art was a consequence of her politicization *as* a Korean-American woman artist. Women artists of color are, it needs hardly be said, doubly affected by mutually reinforcing operations of racism and sexism.

Like most of the artists in the exhibition, Min must negotiate the double bind of what could be termed the hyphenated artist (e.g., woman-artist, black-woman-artist, Asian-American-woman-artist, etc.). To the extent that such an artist excludes the psychic and cultural components of her own formation, she forecloses the specificity of vision and her art; to the extent that she embraces the singularity of her identity, and makes it an

zwischenname." Damit wird—wie in anderen Arbeiten auch—eine Verbindung zwischen den Schwierigkeiten der kulturellen und sprachlichen Dislozierung und dem problematischen Verhältnis von Frauen zu Sprache und Identität nahegelegt.

Yong Soon Min gehört fast genau zur selben Generation wie Cha, die beiden waren Freundinnen in Berkeley, wo sie in den 70er Jahren studierten. Nach Soon Mins eigener Beschreibung ihrer künstlerischen Entwicklung war die Auseinandersetzung mit Fragen der Identität als Gegenstand ihrer Kunst eine Folge ihrer Politisierung *als* koreoamerikanische Künstler*in*. Farbige Künstler*innen* sind, wie man wohl kaum betonen muß, doppelt von den einander verstärkenden Wirkungen von Rassismus und Sexismus betroffen.

Wie die meisten Künstlerinnen in dieser Ausstellung muß Min mit dem Double-bind des sogenannten "zusammengesetzten" Künstlers fertigwerden (Künstler*in*, schwarze Künstler*in*, asiatoamerikanische Künstler*in* usw.). Sofern eine solche Künstlerin die psychischen und kulturellen Komponenten, die sie geprägt haben, ausschließt, verwirft sie von vornherein das Besondere ihres Blicks und ihrer Kunst; sofern sie die Einzigartigkeit ihrer Identität akzeptiert und zu einem integralen Bestandteil ihrer Arbeit macht, gibt sie den geheiligten Boden des "reinen" Künstlers auf. Im Augenblick schafft das Interesse der Kunstwelt am Multikulturalismus die Bedingungen für die Sichtbarkeit des zusammengesetzten Künstlers; aber ob es sich dabei nur um eine vorübergehende Mode handelt oder wirklich um einen grundlegenden Wandel in der Kunstpolitik, läßt sich nicht sagen. Wie dem auch sei, Soon Min hat sich jedenfalls selbst dazu geäußert, was das Eingehen der Kunstproduktion auf die Umstände der asiatoamerikanischen Identität bedeutet:

> ...es steht viel auf dem Spiel, wenn man über die Identität einer marginalisierten Gruppe wie der der Asiatoamerikaner zu sprechen versucht, vor allem wenn es um die Künstler und Kulturarbeiter dieser Gruppe geht, die man in gewisser Weise als doppelt marginalisiert betrachten könnte. Es ist nicht einfach damit getan, die Beschaffenheit und die Merkmale der individuellen und/oder kollektiven Identität von Asiatoamerikanern und deren Kulturproduktion zu beschreiben. Unsere kulturelle Identität ist zu einem immer umstritteneren Gebilde geworden, überflutet von komplexen und gegensätzlichen Führungs-, Besitz- und Authentizitätsansprüchen von zahllosen Seiten, erwarteten wie unerwarteten. Sofern es in den Kämpfen von Menschen aus der dritten Welt hauptsächlich um Landrechte und Selbstbestimmung geht, geht es bei der Bestimmung unserer kulturellen Identität in diesem Land zwangsläufig auch um die Eroberung eines Territotiums—die Beanspruchung eines Ortes und die Behauptung einer Position gegenüber den herrschenden kulturellen Kräften—um unseres eigenen kulturellen Zusammenhalts und Wohlergehens willen.[28]

integral aspect of her artmaking, she cedes the high ground of the unhyphenated designation "artist." At the moment, the art world's embrace of multiculturalism provides the conditions for the hyphenated artist's visibility, but whether this represents the fashion of the moment or a substantive shift in aesthetic politics is impossible to know. In any case, Min has herself written about the implications of adjusting art production to the circumstances of Asian-American identity:

> ...there is much at stake in an attempt to address the identity of a marginalized group such as Asian-Americans and specifically, the artists and the cultural workers of this group who may perhaps be considered to be doubly marginalized. It is not simply a matter of describing the make-up and characteristics of the individual and/or collective identity of Asian-Americans and their cultural production. Our cultural identity has become ever more a contested entity inundated with complex and contradictory claims of authority, authenticity and ownership from a myriad of sources, expected and unexpected. Insofar as much of the primary struggles of Third World people are about land rights and self-determination, our own determination of cultural identity here necessarily also involves a struggle for territory—claiming a place and asserting a position in relation to dominant cultural forces—for our own cultural integrity and well-being.[28]

In the installation excerpted from the work entitled *deCOLONIZATION* (fig. 18a–b), consisting of a seven-foot-long traditional Korean robe and four image/text panels mounted on the wall, Yong Soon Min weaves together the shards of personal history. The presiding metaphors are that of overlay and overlap: the sepia-lettered Korean verse marked on the diaphanous robe, which by virtue of scale is a commanding presence; the dense interweaving of photocopied images with various texts; the "screen" of frosted mylar through which one views three of the panels; and the mix of biographic reminiscence with literary and historic reference. The poem, entitled "Home," is repeated in English translation on the back of the robe.

Whether the semitransparent robe is to be interpreted as synecdoche for motherland and Korean woman, as one curator has suggested, or as emblematic symbol of a Korea that is as much subjective as geographic, is less significant than the palimpsest-like quality of *deCOLONIZATION*'s organization, in which different layers of an elusive and mercurial identity are simultaneously in play. Here too, the concept of identity as bricolage seems apposite, given that Min's deployment of signs of "Koreanness" are at once discrete, decontextualized, aggregate.

In der Installation, die der Arbeit mit dem Titel *deCOLONIZATION* (Fig. 18a–b) entnommen ist und die aus einem über zwei Meter langen traditionellen koreanischen Festgewand und vier an der Wand installierten Bild/Text-Tafeln besteht, setzt Soon Min die Scherben ihrer eigenen Geschichte zusammen. Die vorherrschenden Metaphern sind die der Überlappung und Überlagerung: da sind die sepiaroten koreanischen Verse auf dem transparenten Gewand, das wegen seiner Größe den Raum beherrscht; die dichte Verflechtung von fotokopierten Bildern mit verschiedenen Texten; die "Mattscheibe" aus beschichtetem Mylar, durch die man auf eine der Tafeln blickt; und die Mischung aus biographischen Erinnerungen und literarischen und historischen Bezügen. Das Gedicht mit dem Titel "Home" wird auf der Rückseite des Gewandes in englischer Übersetzung wiedergegeben.

Ob das halbdurchsichtige Gewand nun als Synekdoche für Mutterland und koreanische Frau zu interpretieren ist, wie eine Kuratorin gemeint hat, oder als emblematisches Zeichen für ein Korea, das in gleichem Maße subjektiv wie geographisch ist, ist weniger entscheidend als der palimpsestartige Aufbau der Arbeit, in der verschiedene Schichten einer ungreifbaren, wandelhaften Identität gleichzeitig miteinander im Spiel sind. Auch hier scheint es angemessen, von einem Konzept der Identität als Bricolage zu sprechen—vor allem angesichts dessen, daß Soon Min die Zeichen des "Koreanischen" auf eine Art einsetzt, die diese zugleich für sich stehen läßt, entkontextualisiert und miteinander verknüpft. Und in dem Maße wie *deCOLONIZATION* sich explizit auf einen historischen Prozeß der Selbstbestimmung bezieht, dem selbst wieder die Spuren früherer Beherrschung eingeschrieben sind (im Falle Koreas die Dominanz durch China, Japan und—in Südkorea—die USA), reflektiert die Arbeit auch die stets unvollständigen und vorläufigen Prozesse der Identitätsfindung und Selbstdefinition.

Im weitesten Sinne betrachtet führt das Problem, das sich aus dem Fragemodus ergibt, in dem die Künstler von *Mistaken Identities* die unzähligen Stränge der subalternen, zusammengesetzten oder Weder/Noch-Identitäten präsentieren, zurück auf die Bedingungen der Möglichkeit der politischen Äußerung. Wenn in der künstlerischen Praxis Identitäten in all ihrer historischen Bedingtheit, Mehrdeutigkeit und Unentschiedenheit dargestellt werden—wenn die möglichen Identitäten in all ihrer Konstruiertheit artikuliert werden—, von welcher Basis aus will man dann eine Kunstpolitik betreiben, die Eigenständigkeit und kulturelle Mitbestimmung einfordert und den herrschenden Diskurs in Frage stellt? Gibt es, so könnte man fragen, so etwas wie eine vorläufige Identitätspolitik, etwas wie

EL PLAN DE DELANO

We, the undersigned, gathered in Pilgrimage to the capital of the State in Sacramento, in penance for all the failings of Farm Workers as free and sovereign men, do solemnly declare before the civilized world which judges our actions, and before the nation to which we belong, the propositions we have formulated to end the injustice that oppresses us.

We are conscious of the historical significance of our Pilgrimage. It is clearly evident that our path travels through a valley well known to all Mexican farm workers. We know all of these towns of Delano, Fresno, Madera, Modesto, Stockton, and Sacramento, because along this very same road, in this very same valley the Mexican race has sacrificed itself for the last hundred years. Our sweat and our blood have fallen on this land to make other men rich. Our wages and working conditions have been determined from above, because irresponsible legislators who could have helped us have supported the rancher's argument that the plight of the farm worker was a "special case." They saw the obvious effects of an unjust system, starvation wages, contractors, day hauls, forced migration, sickness, and subhuman conditions.

The farm worker has been abandoned to his own fate—without representation, without power—subject to the mercy and caprice of the rancher.

We are suffering. We have suffered unnumbered ills and crimes in the name of the Law of the land. Our men, women and children have suffered not only the basic brutality of stoop labor, and the most obvious injustices of the system; they have also suffered the desperation of knowing that that system caters to the greed of callous men and not to our needs.

Now we will suffer for the purpose of ending the poverty, the misery, and the injustice, with the hope that our children will not be exploited as we have been. They have imposed hungers on us, and now we hunger for justice. We draw strength from the very despair in which we have been forced to live. WE SHALL ENDURE!

This Pilgrimage is a witness to the suffering we have seen for generations. The penance we accept symbolizes the suffering we shall have in order to bring justice to these same towns, to this same valley. This is the beginning of a social movement in fact and not in pronouncements.

We seek our basic God-given rights as human beings. Because we have suffered—and are not afraid to suffer—in order to survive, we are ready to give up everything, even our lives, in our fight for social justice. We shall do it without violence because that is our destiny.

To the ranchers and to all those who oppose us we say, in the words of Benito Juarez, "Respect for another's rights is the meaning of Peace."

We seek the support of all political groups, and the protection of the government, which is also our government. But we are tired of words, of betrayals, of indifference. To the politicians we say that the years are gone when the farm worker said nothing and did nothing to help himself. From this movement shall spring leaders who shall understand us, lead us, be faithful to us, and we shall elect them to represent us. We shall be heard!

We seek, and have, the support of the Church in what we do. At the head of the Pilgrimage we carry the Virgin of Guadalupe because she is ours, all ours, Patroness of the Mexican people. We also carry the Sacred Cross and the Star of David because we are not sectarians, and because we ask the help and prayers of all religions. All men are brothers, sons of the same God; that is why we say to all men of good will, in the words of Pope Leo XIII, "Everyone's first duty is to protect the workers from the greed of speculators who use human beings as instruments to provide themselves with money. It is neither just nor human to oppress with excessive work to the point where their minds become enfeebled and their bodies worn out." God shall not abandon us!

We shall unite. We have learned the meaning of unity. We know why these United States are just that—united. The strength of the poor is also in union. We know that the poverty of the Mexican or Filipino worker in California is the same as that of all farm workers across the country, the Negroes and poor whites, the Puerto Ricans, Japanese and Arabians; in short, all of the races that compromise the oppressed minorities of the United States. The majority of the people on our Pilgrimage are of Mexican descent, but the triumph of our race depends on a national association of farm workers. We must get together and bargain collectively. We must use the only strength that we have, the force of our numbers; the ranchers are few, we are many. United we shall stand!

We shall pursue the Revolution we have proposed. We are sons of the Mexican Revolution, a revolution of the poor seeking bread and justice. Our revolution shall not be an armed one, but we want the order which now exists to be undone, and that a new social order replace it.

We are poor, we are humble, and our only choice is to Strike in those ranches where we are not treated with the respect we deserve as working men, where our rights as free and sovereign men are not recognized. We do not want the paternalism of the ranchers; we do not want the contractor; we do not want charity at the price of our dignity. We want to be equal with all the working men in the nation; we want a just wage, better working conditions, a decent future for our children. To those who oppose us, be they ranchers, police, politicians, or speculators, we say that we are going to continue fighting until we die, or we win. We shall overcome!

Across the San Joaquin Valley, across California, across the entire Southwest of the United States, wherever there are Mexican people, wherever there are farm workers, our movement is spreading like flames across a dry plain. Our Pilgrimage is the match that will light our cause for all farm workers to see what is happening here, so that they may do as we have done.

The time has come for the liberation of the poor farm worker. History is on our side. May the Strike go on! Viva la causa!

March 1966

Manifesto and public declaration issued in 1966 by Farm Workers connected with the Delano Grape Strike in California, attempting both liberation and reform in farm labor practice, and, seeking social justice and fairness for the farm laborer.

PLAN DE LA RAZA UNIDA

On this historic day, October 28, 1967, La Raza Unida organized in El Paso, Texas, proclaims the time of subjugation, exploitation and abuse of human rights of La Raza in the United States is hereby ended forever.

La Raza Unida affirms the magnificence of La Raza, the greatness of our heritage, our history, our language, our traditions, our contributions to humanity, and our culture. We have demonstrated and proven and again affirm our loyalty to the Constitutional Democracy of the United States of America and to the religious and cultural traditions we all share.

We accept the framework of constitutional democracy and freedom within which to establish our own independent organizations among our own people in pursuit of justice and equality and redress of grievances. La Raza Unida pledges to join with all our courageous people organizing in the fields and in the barrios. We commit ourselves to La Raza, at whatever cost.

With this commitment we pledge our support in:

1. The right to organize community and labor groups in our own style.

2. The guarantee of training and placement in employment at all levels.

3. The guarantee of special emphasis on education at all levels geared to our people with strong financial grants to individuals.

4. The guarantee of decent, safe, and sanitary housing without relocation from one's community.

5. We demand equal representation at all levels of appointive boards and agencies, and the end to exploitative gerrymandering.

6. We demand the strong enforcement of all sections of the Treaty of Guadalupe Hidalgo particularly the sections dealing with land grants, and bilingual guarantees.

7. We are outraged by and demand an end to police harassment, discrimination and brutality inflicted on La Raza, and an end to the kangaroo court system known as juvenile hall. We demand constitutional protection and guarantees in all courts of the United States.

8. We reaffirm a dedication to our heritage, a bilingual culture and assert our right to be members of La Raza Unida anywhere, anytime and in any job.

Declaration of Independence by Chicano political party, "La Raza Unida," formed in the United States border-town of El Paso, Texas by leading members of the Mexican-American intelligentsia.

THE SPIRITUAL PLAN OF AZTLAN

In the spirit of a new people that is conscious not only of its proud heritage, but also of the brutal "gringo" invasion of our territories, we, the Chicano, inhabitants and civilizers of the northern land of Aztlán, from whence came our forefathers, reclaiming the land of their birth and consecrating the determination of our people of the sun, *declare* that the call of our blood is our power, our responsibility, and our inevitable destiny.

We are free and sovereign to determine those tasks which are justly called for by our house, our land, the sweat of our brows, and by our hearts. Aztlán belongs to those that plant the seeds, water the fields, and gather the crops, and not to the foreign Europeans. We do not recognize capricious frontiers on the Bronze Continent.

Brotherhood unites us, love for our brothers makes us a people whose time has come and who struggles against the foreigner "gabacho" who exploits our riches and destroys our culture. With our heart in our hand and our hands in the soil, we declare the independence of our mestizo Nation. We are a bronze people with a bronze culture. Before the world, before all of North America, before all our brothers in the Bronze Continent, we are a Nation. We are a union of free pueblos. We are Aztlán.

To hell with the nothing race.

All power for our people.

March 31, 1969

Public resolution adopted in March 1969 at the first National Chicano Youth Conference (in conjunction with Crusade for Justice Youth Conference), Denver, Colorado.

Fig. 19a
Armando Rascón
Texts from *Artifact with Three Declarations of Independence*
1991

And to the degree that *deCOLONIZATION* makes explicit reference to an historic process of self-determination which is nevertheless inscribed with the traces of prior domination (in the case of Korea, by China, by Japan, and, in South Korea, by the U.S.), it reflects as well on the always partial and provisional processes of self-fashioning and self-definition.

Considered in its broadest terms, the problem posed by the interrogative mode in which the artists in *Mistaken Identities* set out the myriad skeins of subaltern, hyphenated, or neither/nor identities returns to the conditions of political utterance. If, within art practices, identities are presented in all their contingency, ambiguity, irresolution—if the range of possible identities are articulated in all their constructedness—where are the grounds from which to launch an aesthetic politics of entitlement, cultural enfranchisement, and contestation? Is there, one may ask, something like a provisional identity politics, something akin to Gayatri Chakravorty Spivak's "strategic Gayatri Chakravorty Spivaks "strategischen Essentialismus", etwas, das je nach den Umständen in Anspruch genommen werden kann—ähnlich dem Baldwinschen Gewand der Identität—gleichzeitig aber heterogene und multiple Identitäten zuläßt, die doch genauso zum Bereich des Selbst gehören?

Für Minderheiten ist die Erlangung von Selbstrepräsentation zweifellos ein politisches Muß; die Praktiken der bildenden Kunst sind dabei nur ein Aspekt. Der Akt der Selbstbenennung ist in dieser Hinsicht eine entscheidende, emanzipatorische Handlung. Nehmen wir zum Beispiel Norma Alarcóns Erörterung der politischen Implikationen der Bezeichnung Chicana:

> Die Bezeichnung "Chicana" ist nichts, womit Frauen (oder Männer) zur Welt kommen, wie es gewöhnlich bei der Bezeichnung "Mexikanerin" der Fall ist; sie wird vielmehr ganz bewußt und in kritischer Absicht angenommen und dient als Ausgangspunkt für einen erneuten Anlauf, den tradierten Knäuel von Krisen, Verwirrungen, historischen und ideologischen Konflikten und Widersprüchen aufzulösen, der dadurch zustandekommt, daß man gleichzeitig "keinen Namen hat", "viele Namen hat", "seinen

Fig. 19b
Armando Rascón
Artifact with Three Declarations of Independence, 1991
installation view
Cat. no. 16

essentialism" that can be circumstantially claimed, like Baldwin's garment of identity, but which allows for the heterogeneity and multiple identifications that are equally the province of the individual self?

Clearly it is a political imperative for dominated groups to achieve self-representation, of which visual cultural practices are but one element. In this respect, the act of self-naming is a crucial and empowering activity. Consider, for example, Norma Alarcón's discussion of the political modalities inhering in the name Chicana:

> The name Chicana is not a name that women (or men) are born with, as is often the case with "Mexican," but rather it is consciously and critically assumed and serves as point of redeparture for dismantling historical conjunctures of crisis, confusion, political and ideological conflict and contradictions of the simultaneous effects of having "no names," having "many names," not "know(ing) her names," and being someone else's "dreamwork." However, digging into the historically despised dark (prieto) body in strictly psychological terms, may get her back to the bare bones and marrow, but she may not "find the way back," to writing her embodied histories. The idea of plural historicized bodies is proposed with respect to the multiple racial constructions of the body since "the discovery."[29]

It is in relation to both my rhetorical questions and to the implications of Alarcón's text, that I close with a consideration of Armando Rascón's *Artifact with Three Declarations of Independence* (fig. 19a–b).

Assembled here are twelve "found"photographs, framed as found, including dust and marks of age and neglect. With the exception of the four portrait snapshots, the pictures consist of familiar stereotypes of "Mexicanness"—the bullfight, the "native" market, the grizzled campesino, the richly adorned señorita, the Zorro-like silhouette, and so forth. Below are mounted the three declarations of the installation's title, manifestos respectively of "El Plan de Delano of 1966" (the founding statement of the Delano Grape Strike, formulated by the nascent Farm Workers Union), the 1967 preamble of the "Plan de la Raza Unida" (the declaration of independence by the Chicano political party "La Raza Unida," formed in the Texas border town of El Paso), and "The Spiritual Plan of Aztlan" of 1969 (a public resolution adopted at the First National Chicano Youth Conference in conjunction with the Crusade for Justice Youth Conference in Denver, Colorado).

These manifestos represent three political moments in the formation of a Chicano political identity and consciousness and three discrete moments of political

Namen nicht kennt" und "von jemand anderem geträumt" wird. Wenn sich eine mit dem historisch verachteten dunkelhäutigen (prieto) Körper in rein psychologischer Hinsicht beschäftigt, mag sie zwar zu ihrem nackten Kern finden, aber sie wird dann vielleicht nicht "wieder zurückfinden", um ihre verkörperten Geschichten zu schreiben. Der Vorschlag, den Körper vielfältig zu historisieren, erfolgt angesichts der multiplen rassischen Konstruktionen des Körpers seit "der Entdeckung".[29]

Sowohl wegen des Bezugs zu meinen rhetorischen Fragen als auch wegen der Implikationen von Alarcóns Text schließe ich mit einer Betrachtung von Armando Rascóns *Artifact with Three Declarations of Independence* (Fig. 19a–b).

Die Arbeit besteht aus einem Arrangement von zwölf "gefundenen" Fotografien in genau dem Zustand gerahmt, wie sie vorgefunden wurden, verstaubt und von Alter und sorglosem Umgang gezeichnet. Mit Ausnahme der vier Porträtfotos zeigen die Bilder wohlbekannte Stereotypen des "Mexikanischen"—den Stierkampf, den "einheimischen" Markt, den ergrauten Campesino, die reichgeschmückte Señorita, die Zorro-Silhouette usw. Darunter sind die drei im Titel erwähnten Unabhängigkeitserklärungen angebracht, nämlich: "El Plan de Delano" aus dem Jahre 1966 (das Gründungsmanifest der anläßlich des Traubenpflückerstreiks von Delano entstandenen Farmarbeitergewerkschaft), die 1967er Präambel zum "Plan de la Raza Unida" (die Unabhängigkeitserklärung der Chicano-Partei "La Raza Unida", gegründet in der texanischen Grenzstadt El Paso) und der "Spiritual Plan of Aztlan" aus dem Jahre 1969 (eine Resolution, verabschiedet von der ersten nationalen Chicano-Jugendkonferenz, welche im Zusammenhang mit der Jugendkonferenz "Crusade for Justice" in Denver, Colorado, abgehalten wurde).

Diese Manifeste repräsentieren drei politische Bewegungen, die für die Bildung einer politischen Identität und eines politischen Bewußtseins der Chicanos eine Rolle spielten, und zugleich auch drei aufeinanderfolgende Phasen ihrer politischen Organisation. Sie dokumentieren für den Zeitraum der drei Jahre, in denen sie stattgefunden haben, eine Evolution von einer Politik, die zutiefst religös inspiriert war (unter der Schirmherrschaft der Hl. Jungfrau von Guadalupe), bis hin zur Ausrufung eines "bronzenen Volkes" mit einer eigenen "Bronzekultur", die sich auf den Aztlan-Mythos gründet.[30] Die Manifeste dokumentieren aber auch die Entwicklung von einer Sprache des Leidens und der Unterwürfigkeit ("wir sind arme, bescheidene Leute und uns bleibt nur die Wahl, jene Farmen zu bestreiken, die uns nicht mit dem Respekt behandeln, der uns als arbeitenden Menschen gebürt...") zur Verächtlichkeit und Militanz der Chicano-Jugendkonferenz ("Zur Hölle mit der Nichtsrasse. Alle Macht unserem Volk").

organization. They trace, in the three-year period of their appearance, an evolution from a politics profoundly informed by religious piety, presided over by the Virgin of Guadalupe, to the affirmation of a "bronze people" with a "bronze culture," whose presiding myth is that of Aztlan.[30] The declarations trace as well a transition from a discourse of suffering and humility ("we are poor, we are humble, and our only choice is to strike in those ranches where we are not treated with the respect we deserve as working men...") to the defiance and militancy of the Chicano Youth Conference ("to hell with the nothing race. All power for our people.").

Counterpointed in Rascón's installation is, on the one hand, the image world of cultural stereotype—what could be called the Gringo imaginary—mingled with modest, vernacular examples of self-representation (such as the snapshot portrait of the campesino couple)—and on the other, the actual process of political articulation and political/cultural self-definition. It is the space *between* these two representational "sets" that can be said to constitute the viewer's share. This space operates as a kind of discursive ellipsis, dividing the domain of conventional and stereotypic representation (in which the Chicano or Mexican exists as object) from the declarations of political agency, in which the participants collectively assert their identity as subjects. Hence, for the non-Chicano/a the instrumentality of *Artifact with Three Declarations of Independence* resides in how the viewer positions him/herself in relation to both the familiar cultural fantasy and the textual documentation of political struggle—"the subaltern speaks." Where so much previous postmodern art practice assumed that quotation or appropriation could in itself dissolve the ossified accretions of political and cultural myth, Rascón, like the other artists in *Mistaken Identities*, instates the historical real, the uneven, erratic but potentially transforming activity of political organization, contestation, and continual struggle that is a catalyst of new identities in the making.

Was Rascóns Installation miteinander konfrontiert, ist zum einen die Bildwelt des kulturellen Stereotyps—das, was man als Gringo-Imagination bezeichnen könnte—vermischt mit bescheidenen, volkstümlichen Beispielen der Selbstrepräsentation (wie etwa dem Schnappschuß des Campesinopaars) und andererseits der tatsächliche Prozeß der politischen Artikulation und der politisch-kulturellen Selbstdefinition. Man kann sagen, daß der Raum *zwischen* diesen beiden Repräsentationsweisen den Anteil des Betrachters ausmacht. Dieser Raum fungiert als eine Art diskursiver Leerstelle, die den Bereich der konventionellen und stereotypen Darstellung (in der der Chicano oder Mexikaner zum Objekt wird) von den Dokumenten der politischen Aktion trennt, in denen die Teilnehmer gemeinsam ihre Identität als Subjekte artikulieren. Für Nicht-Chicanos liegt daher die Funktion von "Artifact with Three Declarations of Independence" darin, daß sie sich klarwerden müssen, wie sie sich als Zuschauer zwischen der vertrauten kulturellen Vorstellung und der Textdokumentation des politischen Kampfes ("der Subalterne meldet sich zu Wort") positionieren. Wo die frühere postmoderne Praxis vielfach davon ausging, daß Zitat und Appropriation allein schon die verknöcherten Anhäufungen politischer und kultureller Mythen zersetzen könnten, setzt Rascon—wie die anderen Künstler in *Mistaken Identities* auch—das historisch Reale ein, die auf und ab schwankende, hin und her irrende, aber potentiell verändernde Aktivität der politischen Organisation, der Infragestellung und des unablässigen Kampfes—eine Aktivität, die ein Katalysator ist für neue Identitäten im Prozeß ihrer Entstehung.

ENDNOTES

1. Adrienne Rich, *Blood, Bread and Poetry* (New York: W.W. Norton, 1986).

2. The original formulation of this concept of "marking" is Monique Wittig's. See her important essay, "The Mark of Gender," in Monique Wittig, *The Straight Mind and Other Essays*, foreword by Louise Turcotte (Boston: Beacon Press, 1992), 76–89.

3. See, for example, Judith Wilson's incisive critique of the exclusions in postmodern art theory, especially in Craig Owens' much-cited essay, "The Discourse of Others: Feminism and Postmodernism," in Hal Foster, ed., *The Anti-Aesthetic: Essays on Post-Modern Culture* (Port Townsend, Wash.: Bay Press, 1983), 57–82. Wilson (and other critics) have pointed out that while postmodernist theorists make much of the new ascendancy of non-Western nations and cultures and the concomitant eclipse of the West and its master narratives of dominance and legitimation, the language of culture and its most privileged representatives remain, for the most part, obdurately white, Western, and male. See too Judith Wilson,"Seventies into Eighties-Neo-Hoodoo-ism vs. Postmodernism: When (Art) Worlds Collide," in *The Decade Show: Frameworks of Identity in the 1980s*, exhibition catalog (New York: Museum of Contemporary Hispanic Art, The New Museum of Contemporary Art, The Studio Museum in Harlem, 1990).

4. Rasheed Araeen, "Our Bauhaus, Others' Mudhouse," *Third Text*, No. 6 (1989). Cited in Jimmie Durham, "A Central Margin," in *The Decade Show*, *op. cit.*, 168.

5. In addition to being an artist, Piper is an academically trained philosopher. As a philosopher, her primary intellectual influence (and current project) is Kantian. Most postmodernist theory, on the contrary, takes its cues from the tradition of Nietzsche, and in the twentieth century, from Heidegger. See Maurice Berger, "The Critique of Pure Racism: An Interview with Adrian Piper," *Afterimage* 10, no. 3 (October 1990), 5–9.

6. Sarat Maharaj, "The Congo is Flooding the Acropolis: Black Art, Orders of Difference, Textiles," in *Interrogating Identity*, exhibition catalog (New York: Grey Art Gallery and Study Center, 1991), 15.

7. When an exhibition of Weems' work which included the *Jokes* series was shown in Halifax, Canada, an angry protest was organized by black students at Dalhousie University.

8. This in a colonial context. See Homi Bhabha, "The Other Question— The Stereotype and Colonial Discourse," *Screen* 24 (November–December 1983), 18–36; and Homi Bhabha, "Of Mimicry and Man: The Ambivalence of Colonial Discourse," *October* 28 (Spring 1984), 125–33.

9. Henry Louis Gates, Jr., *The Signifying Monkey: A Theory of Afro-American Literary Criticism* (New York: Oxford University Press, 1988).

10. While photography is conventionally considered a realist medium, especially in its strictly informational or communicative uses, its deployment by the artists in the exhibition is obviously far removed from documentary or purely descriptive applications.

11. Orlando Patterson, *Slavery and Social Death* (Cambridge: Harvard University Press, 1982).

12. Adrian Piper, "Xenophobia and the Indexical Present," in Mark O'Brien and Craig Little, eds., *Reimaging America: The Arts of Social Change* (Philadelphia: New Society Publishers, 1990), 288–9.

13. Drucilla Cornell, *Beyond Accommodation: Ethical Feminism, Deconstruction and the Law* (New York: Routledge, 1991), 5.

14. Ralph Ellison, *The Invisible Man* (New York: Random House, 1952). See too Michele Wallace's discussion in *Invisibility Blues: From Pop to Theory* (London: Verso, 1990).

ANMERKUNGEN

1. Adrienne Rich, *Blood, Bread and Poetry*, New York: W. W. Norton, 1986.

2. Das Konzept der "Markierung" wurde ursprünglich von Monique Wittig formuliert. Vgl. ihren wichtigen Essay, "The Mark of Gender", in: M. W., *The Straight Mind and Other Essays*, Foreword by Louise Turcotte, Boston: Beacon Press, 1992, S. 76–89.

3. Vgl. beispielsweise Judith Wilsons einschneidende Kritik der Ausgrenzungen der postmodernen Kunsttheorie—besonders in Craig Owens vielzitiertem Aufsatz, "The Discourse of Others: Feminism and Postmodernism", in: Hal Foster (Hg.), *The Anti-Aesthetic: Essays on Post-Modern Culture,* Port Townsend, Wash.: Bay Press, 1983, S. 57–82. Wie Wilson (und andere Kritiker/innen) gezeigt haben, beziehen sich postmoderne Theoretiker zwar stark auf den Aufstieg nicht-westlicher Nationen und Kulturen und den damit einhergehenden Niedergang des Westens und seiner legitimatorischen Herrschaftsnarrative, aber die Sprache der Kultur und ihre privilegiertesten Repräsentanten bleiben zum Großteil hartnäckig weiß, westlich und männlich. Vgl. Judith Wilson, "Seventies into Eighties-Neo-Hoodoo-ism vs. Postmodernism: When (Art) Worlds Collide", in: *The Decade Show: Frameworks of Identity in the 1980's* (Ausstellungskatalog), New York: Museum of Contemporary Hispanic Art, The New Museum of Contemporary Art, The Studio Museum in Harlem, 1990.

4. Rasheed Araeen, "Our Bauhaus, Others' Mudhouse", in: *Third Text*, Nr. 6 (1989), zitiert nach Jimmie Durham, "A Central Margin", in: *The Decade Show*, S. 168.

5. Piper ist nicht nur Künstlerin, sondern auch eine akademisch ausgebildete Philosophin. Als solche sind ihre Einflüsse (und ihr gegenwärtiges philosophisches Projekt) hauptsächlich kantianisch. Die postmoderne Theorie hingegen bezieht sich zumeist auf die Tradition Nietzsches und—im 20. Jahrhundert— Heideggers. Vgl. Maurice Berger, "The Critique of Pure Racism: An Interview with Adrian Piper", in: *Afterimage*, Bd. 10, Nr. 3 (Oktober 1990), S. 5–9.

6. Sarat Maharaj, "The Congo is Flooding the Acropolis: Black Art, Orders of Difference, Textiles", in: *Interrogating Identity,* Ausstellungskatalog, New York: Gray Art Gallery and Study Center, 1991, S. 15.

7. Bei einer Ausstellung von Weems' Arbeiten in Halifax, Kanada, bei der auch ihre Serie *Jokes* zu sehen war, organisierten schwarze Studenten von der Dalhousie Universität einen zornigen Protest.

8. Und zwar in einem kolonialen Kontext. Vgl. Homi Bhabha, "The Other Question—The Stereotype and Colonial Discourse", in: *Screen* 24 (November–Dezember 1983), S. 18–36; und Homi Bhabha, "Of Mimicry and Man: The Ambivalence of Colonial Discourse", in *October* 28 (Frühjahr 1984), S. 125–133.

9. Henry Louis Gates Jr., *The Signifying Monkey: A Theory of Afro-American Literary Criticism*, New York: Oxford University Press, 1988.

10. Entgegen der konventionellen Auffassung von Fotografie als einem realistischen Medium—vor allem in ihren streng informativen und kommunikativen Verwendungsformen—wird sie von den Künstlern dieser Ausstellung auf eine Art gebraucht, die von dokumentarischen oder rein deskriptiven Verwendungsweisen offensichtlich weit entfernt ist.

11. Orlando Patterson, *Slavery and Social Death*, Cambridge: Harvard University Press, 1982.

12. Adrian Piper, "Xenophobia and the Indexical Present", in: Mark O'Brien and Craig Little (Hg.), *Reimaging America: The Arts of Social Change*, Philadelphia: New Society Publishers, 1990, S. 288–289.

13. Drucilla Cornell, *Beyond Accommodation: Ethical Feminism, Deconstruction and the Law,* New York: Routledge, 1991, S. 5.

14. Ralph Ellison, *The Invisible Man,* New York: Random House, 1952. Vgl. auch die Erörterung von Michele Wallace in: *Invisibility Blues: From Pop to Theory,* London: Verso, 1990.

15. It is worth noting that in 1980 Piper produced a sound/image installation entitled *Four Intruders Plus Alarm Systems* in which the illuminated faces of four black men, larger than life size, were installed in a small dark room. An audio track on earphones relayed the responses of fictional viewers, which were primarily racist in nature.

16. See Coco Fusco's excellent discussion of Simpson's work, "Uncanny Dissonance: The Work of Lorna Simpson," in *Lorna Simpson*, exhibition catalog (Hamilton, N.Y.: The Gallery of the Department of Art and Art History, Dana Arts Center, Colgate University, November–December, 1991).

17. The analysis of femininity in relation to specularity and the privileging of the visual is most immediately associated with the earlier work of Luce Irigaray. See *Speculum of the Other Woman*, translated by Catherine Porter (Ithaca: Cornell University Press, 1985). See too Sarah Kofman, *The Enigma of Woman*, translated by Catherine Porter (Ithaca: Cornell University Press, 1985).

18. This allusive characterization is Patricia Williams'. See her brilliant *The Alchemy of Race and Rights: Diary of a Law Professor* (Cambridge: Harvard University Press, 1991).

19. In Britain there is a tendency to consider all of those who are not of obvious European ancestry as "colored"; hence, there has emerged a political counter-tactic wherein all those thus designated affirm their identity as "black." In political, if not in racial terms, Tabrizian makes common cause with British women of color.

20. One of Victor Burgin's essays makes a provocative case for the applicability of dreamwork mechanisms to the mechanisms and spectatorial address of photographic imagery. See "Photography, Phantasy, Function," in Burgin, ed., *Thinking Photography* (London: Macmillan, 1986).

21. Judith Wilson, "In Memory of the News and of Our Selves: The Art of Adrian Piper," *Third Text* 16/17 (Autumn/Winter 1991), 62. Wilson's detailed, thoughtful account of Piper's work from the '70s to the present provides the best and most thorough discussion to date.

22. Hortense Spillers, "Notes on an Alternative Model: Neither/Nor," in Mike Davis, Manning Marable, Fred Pfeil, and Michael Sprinker, eds., *The Near Left 2: Toward a Rainbow Socialism* (London: Verso, 1987), 176.

23. Guillermo Gómez-Peña, "On Nationality: Thirteen Artists," *Art in America* 79, no. 9 (September 1991), 126.

24. Guillermo Gómez-Peña, "Border Culture: The Multicultural Paradigm," in *The Decade Show*, op cit., 97.

25. See Jimmie Durham, "Cowboys and...Notes on Art, Literature, and American Indians in the Modern American Mind," in Annette Jaimes, ed., *The State of Native America* (Boston: South End Press, 1992), 423–438.

26. Cited in Jean Fisher, "Jimmie Durham," in *Jimmie Durham: The Bishop's Moose and the Pinkerton Men*, exhibition catalog (New York: Exit Art, 1989), 12.

27. Cha's extant work is in the collections of the University Art Museum/Pacific Film Archive, University of California, Berkeley.

28. Yong Soon Min, "Territorial Waters: Mapping Asian American Cultural Identity," *Harbour* 1, no. 2 (1990), 34.

29. Norma Alarcón, "Chicana Feminism: In the Tracks of 'The' Native Woman," *Cultural Studies* 4, no. 3 (October 1990), 250.

30. For a Chicana reading of the Chicana movement, especially in relation to the symbolics of the Virgin of Guadalupe, see Angie Chabram-Dernersesian, "I Throw Punches for My Race, but I Don't Want to Be a Man: Writing Us—Chica-nos(Girls, Us)/Chica*nas*—Into the Movement Script," in Lawrence Grossberg, Cary Nelson, Paula Treichler, eds., *Cultural Studies* (New York: Routledge, 1992), 81–95.

15. Es ist in diesem Zusammenhang aufschlußreich, daß Piper 1980 eine Ton/Bild-Installation mit dem Titel *Four Intruders Plus Alarm Systems* produzierte, bei der in einem kleinen, dunklen Raum die erleuchteten, überlebensgroßen Gesichter von vier schwarzen Männern installiert waren. Von Tonband wurden über Kopfhörer die vorwiegend rassistischen Reaktionen fiktiver Betrachter zugespielt.

16. Vgl. Coco Fuscos ausgezeichneten Essay über Simpsons Arbeit "Uncanny Dissonance: The Work of Lorna Simpson", in: *Lorna Simpson* (Ausstellungskatalog) Hamilton, N.Y.: The Gallery of the Department of Art and Art History, Dana Arts Center, Colgate University, November–Dezember 1991.

17. Die Analyse des Weiblichen im Zusammenhang mit Sichtbarkeit und der Privilegierung des Visuellen wird am ehesten verbunden mit dem frühen Werk von Luce Irrigaray, vgl. ihr *Speculum. Der weibliche Diskurs*, aus d. Franz. v. Xenia Rajewsky u.a., Frankfurt/M.: Suhrkamp 1980. Vgl. auch Sarah Kofman, *The Enigma of Woman*, transl. by Catherine Porter, Ithaca: Cornell University Press, 1985.

18. Diese suggestive Charakterisierung stammt von Patricia Williams. Vgl. ihr brillantes Buch, *The Alchemy of Race and Rights: Diary of a Law Professor,* Cambridge: Harvard University Press, 1991.

19. In Großbritannien besteht die Tendenz, alle, die nicht eindeutig europäischer Abstammung sind, als "colored" zu bezeichnen, weshalb sich die politische Gegentaktik entwickelt hat, daß sich alle derart Etikettierten als "black" identifizieren. Tabrizian stellt sich damit in politischer, wenn nicht rassischer Hinsicht in eine Front mit "farbigen" britischen Frauen.

20. In einem seiner Essays schlägt Victor Burgin eine provokative Bresche für die Anwendbarkeit von Mechanismen der Traumarbeit auf die Mechanismen fotografischer Bilder und deren Wirkung auf den Betrachter. Vgl. "Photography, Phantasy, Funktion", in: Victor Burgin (Hg.), *Thinking Photography*, London: Macmillan, 1986.

21. Judith Wilson, "In Memory of the News and of Our Selves: The Art of Adrian Piper", in: *Third Text* 16/17 (Herbst/Winter 1991). Wilsons ausführliche und gedankenvolle Abhandlung über Pipers Arbeit von den 70er Jahren bis heute ist die bisher beste und gründlichste Erörterung.

22. Hortense Spillers, "Notes on an Alternative Model: Neither/Nor", in: Mike Davis, Manning Marable, Fred Pfeil and Michael Sprinker (Hg.), *The Near Left 2: Toward a Rainbow Socialism,* London: Verso, 1987, S. 176.

23. Guillermo Gómez-Peña, "On Nationality: Thirteen Artists", in: *Art in America,* September 1991, S. 126.

24. Guillermo Gómez-Peña, "Border Culture: The Multicultural Paradigm", in: *The Decade Show*, S. 97.

25. Vgl. Jimmie Durham, "Cowboys and...Notes on Art, Literature, and American Indians in the Modern American Mind", in: Annette Jaimes (Hg.), *The State of Native America*, Boston: South End Press, 1992, S. 423–438.

26. Zitiert in Jean Fischer, "Jimmie Durham", in: *Jimmie Durham: The Bishop's Moose and the Pinkerton Men* (Ausstellungskatalog), New York: Exit Art, 1989, S. 12.

27. Chas Nachlaß befindet sich im Pacific Film Archive und University Art Museum, University of California in Berkeley.

28. Yong Soon Min, "Territorial Waters: Mapping Asian American Cultural Identity", in: *Harbour*, Bd. 1, Nr. 2 (1990), S. 34.

29. Norma Alarcón, "Chicana Feminism: In the Tracks of The Native Woman", in: *Cultural Studies*, Bd. 4, Nr. 3 (Oktober 1990), S. 250.

30. Zu einer weiblichen Sicht der Chicano-Bewegung vor allem hinsichtlich der Symbolik der Hl. Jungfrau von Guadalupe vgl. Angie Chabram-Dernersesian, "I Throw Punches for My Race, but I Don't Want to Be a Man: Writing Us—Chica-nos (Girls, Us)/Chica*nas*—Into the Movement Script", in: *Cultural Studies*, Hrsg. v. Lawrence Grossberg, Cary Nelson, Paula Treichler, New York: Routledge, 1992, S. 81–95.

Catalogue of the Exhibition / Ausstellungskatalog

Unless otherwise indicated, dimensions are in inches; height precedes width precedes depth. All photographs are courtesy of the lenders, except where noted.

JIMMIE DURHAM

1. *Bedia's Stirring Wheel*, 1985
   Fabric, leather, steel, stone, mixed materials
   49 x 25 x 17
   Courtesy of the artist and Nicole Klagsbrun Gallery
   New York
   Fig. 16 Photo: Anthony Peres

2. *New Clear Family*, 1989
   Wood, bronze, beads, rope, paint, mixed materials
   19 dolls, each approx. 18 H; overall approx. 86 x 52
   Courtesy of the artist and Nicole Klagsbrun Gallery
   New York
   Fig. 1

3. *A Man Looking for a Place*, 1991
   Photo, wood, metal, mixed materials
   68 x 42 x 25
   Courtesy of the artist and Nicole Klagsbrun Gallery
   New York

CONNIE HATCH

4. *Some Americans: Forced to Disappear*, from *A Display of Visual Inequity*, 1990–91
   Photo-text installation: 12 black and white transparencies in acrylite, l4 x 11; 12 briefing sheets, 11 x 8½; and 2 floor-mounted light boxes, 19 x 59½ x 12; overall dimensions variable
   Courtesy of the artist and Roy Boyd Gallery
   Santa Monica, CA
   Fig. 12

5. From *History on Ice: Distortion Series (after Durer)*
   1990–91
   Two black and white photographs in acrylite, glass block
   4¾ x 18 x 3½
   Collection of Mrs. Charles Ullman

6. From *History on Ice: Distortion Series (Factory)*
   1990–91
   Black and white photograph in acrylite, glass block
   4¾ x 9 x 3½
   Collection of Tania Modleski

MARY KELLY

7. *Menacé*, from *Corpus*, 1984–5
   Part I of the project *Interim*, 1984–9
   Laminated photo positive, silkscreen, and acrylic on Plexiglas
   6 panels, each 48 x 36¼ x 2
   Courtesy of Postmasters Gallery, New York
   Fig. 10 Photo: Anthony Peres

GLENN LIGON

8. *Study for Untitled (I Feel Most Colored)*, 1990
   Oilstick on canvas
   30 x 20
   Collection of Bill Arning and Patrick Owens
   New York

9. *Study for Frankenstein #1*, 1992
   Oilstick on paper
   30 x 15
   Courtesy of The Bohen Foundation, New York

10. *Baldwin #4 (Identity Would Seem...)*, 1992
    Oil and acrylic on black paper
    36½ x 22
    Lent by the artist; courtesy Max Protetch Gallery
    New York
    Fig. 7 Photo: Anthony Peres

YONG SOON MIN

11. From *deCOLONIZATION*, 1991
    Mixed media on dress, mylar, and paper
    Garment, 84 x 48 x 15; four panels, 42 x 25½ each
    Courtesy of the artist
    Fig. 18 Photo: Karen Bell

ADRIAN PIPER

12. *My Calling (Card) #1*, 1986
    Commercial printing on paper
    Each 2 x 3½
    Courtesy of John Weber Gallery, New York
    Fig. 6

13. *Cornered*, 1988
    Video installation with videotape, monitor, table, birth certificates, and chairs
    Approx. 69 x 84 x 164
    Collection of Museum of Contemporary Art
    Chicago, Bernice and Kenneth Newberger Fund
    Fig. 14 Photo: Fred Scruton

14. *Why Guess? #2*, 1989
    Two photo-text collages
    Overall 36 x 59¾
    Courtesy of John Weber Gallery, New York

15. *Why Guess? #4*, 1989
    Two photo-text collages
    Overall 36 x 53⅛
    Courtesy of John Weber Gallery, New York

ARMANDO RASCON

16. *Artifact with Three Declarations of Independence*, 1991
Wood, Plexiglas, found photographs, and three texts:
El Plan de Delano (1966); Plan de La Raza Unida
Preamble (1967); The Spiritual Plan of Aztlán (1969)
Overall approx. 72 x 58
Courtesy of the Artist
Fig. 19

LORNA SIMPSON

17. *Dividing Lines*, 1989
Two color polaroids with 8 plastic plaques
Overall 42¾ x 56
Rubell Family Collections
Fig. 9 Photo: Anthony Peres

18. *Kid Gloves*, 1989
Five color polaroids with 5 plastic plaques
31 x 135
Collection of Catherine Woodard and Nelson Blitz, Jr.
(Santa Barbara only)

19. *H.S.*, 1992, edition 5/5
Two color polaroids with engraved Plexiglas
49½ x 20½
Susan and Michael Hort Collection
Fig. 2

20. *Lower Region*, 1992, edition 1/4
Three color polaroids with engraved Plexiglas
25 x 60½
Courtesy of the artist and Josh Baer Gallery, New York

MITRA TABRIZIAN AND ANDY GOLDING

21. From *The Blues*, 1986–87
Cibachrome photographs, first two of three triptychs
Each panel 49 x 66
Courtesy of the artists
(Because of space limitations, only two of the three
triptychs are exhibited.)
Fig. 11

CARRIE MAE WEEMS

22. *What Are The Three Things You Can't Give A
Black Person?*, from *Ain't Joking*, 1987
Gelatin silver print, with two engraved plastic
plaques and sliding frame
20 x 16
Courtesy of P.P.O.W. Gallery, New York

23. *Black Woman with Chicken*, 1987
Gelatin silver print
20 x 16
Courtesy of P.P.O.W. Gallery, New York
Fig. 4

24. *Four Women*, 1988
Four sepia-toned gelatin silver prints and text
Each 20 x 16
Courtesy of P.P.O.W. Gallery, New York
Fig. 3

PAT WARD WILLIAMS

25. *What you lookn at?*, 1992
Mixed media on photostat
96 x 192
Courtesy of the artist
Fig. 8 Photo: Anthony Peres

Video Program

THERESA HAK KYUNG CHA

26. *Mouth to Mouth*, 1975
Videotape, 8 min.
Collection of the University Art Museum and Pacific
Film Archive, University of California, Berkeley
Gift of the Theresa Hak Kyung Cha Memorial
Foundation

27. *Exilée*, 1978
Videotape, 50 min.
Collection of the University Art Museum and Pacific
Film Archive, University of California, Berkeley
Gift of the Theresa Hak Kyung Cha Memorial
Foundation
Fig. 17

GUILLERMO GOMEZ-PENA

28. *Border Brujo* [Shaman], 1990
Videotape, 52 min.
Fig. 15 Photo: Max Aguilera-Helweg

MARLON RIGGS

30. *Tongues Untied*, 1989
Videotape, 55 min.
Fig. 5 Photo courtesy of Frameline

MARTHA ROSLER

29. *Vital Statistics of a Citizen, Simply Obtained*, 1978
Videotape, 40 min.
Fig. 13 Photo courtesy of the artist

Biographies / Biographien
Bibliographies / Bibliographien

Since 1982 / Seit 1982

NOTE:
1. Where an exhibition has multiple venues, only the originating venue is usually given.
2. Bibliographic citations, catalogs, and exhibitions were selected according to their relevance to the overarching theme of identity.
3. Solo exhibitions, when known, are designated with an asterisk [*].

ANMERKUNG:
1. Bei Ausstellungen, die an mehreren Orten gezeigt wurden, wird gewöhnlich nur der ursprüngliche Ausstellungsort angegeben.
2. Die bibliographischen Angaben, Kataloge und Ausstellungen wurden nach ihrer Relevanz für das übergreifende Identitäts-Thema ausgewählt.
3. Einzelausstellungen, sofern bekannt, sind mit einem Sternchen [*] gekennzeichnet.

THERESA HAK KYUNG CHA

Born Pusan, Korea, 1951
Died New York, 1982

Selected Exhibitions

1989
*Mills College Art Gallery, Oakland
Autobiography: In Her Own Image, INTAR Gallery, New York

1984
Difference: On Representation and Sexuality, New Museum of Contemporary Art, New York

1983
Artists Space, New York

1982
The Kitchen, New York
Athol McBean Gallery, San Francisco Art Institute
Kijkhuis, The Haag, Netherlands
Nova Scotia College of Art and Design, Halifax, Canada

1981
Stedelijk Museum, Amsterdam
Living Museum, Reykjavik, Iceland
*Queens Museum, New York

Selected Bibliography

Barry, Judith. "Women, Representation, and Performance Art: Northern California," in Carl E. Loeffler and Darlene Tong, *Performance Anthology: A Source Book for a Decade of California Performance Art.* San Francisco: Contemporary Arts Press, 1980.

Cha, Theresa Hak Kyung. "Clio/History," in Brian Wallis, ed. *Blasted Allegories: An Anthology of Writings by Contemporary Artists.* New York: New Museum of Contemporary Art, 1987.

_____. "Untitled," in Reese Williams, ed. *Fire Over Water.* New York: Tanam Press, 1986.

_____. *Dictée.* New York: Tanam Press, 1982.

_____. "Exilée Temps Morts," in Reese Williams, ed. *Hotel.* New York: Tanam Press, 1980.

_____. *Apparatus: Cinematographic Apparatus.* New York: Tanam Press, 1980.

_____. *Etang.* Berkeley: Lane, 1979.

The First Annual Asian American International Video Festival (exhibition catalog). San Francisco, 1982.

Lippard, Lucy. *Mixed Blessings: New Art in a Multicultural America.* New York: Pantheon, 1990.

Martin, Stephen-Paul. "Theresa Cha: Creating a Feminine Voice," in *Open Form and the Feminine Imagination: The Politics of Reading in Twentieth-Century Innovative Writing.* Washington, DC: Maisonneuve Press, 1988.

Roth, Moira. "Toward a History of California Performance," *Arts Magazine,* February, 1978.

Stephens, Michael. "Theresa Hak Kyung Cha," in *The Dramaturgy of Style: Voice in Short Fiction.* Carbondale: Southern Illinois University Press, 1986.

Trinh, Minh-ha T. "Grandma's Story," in Brian Wallis, ed. *Blasted Allegories: An Anthology of Writings by Contemporary Artists.* New York: New Museum of Contemporary Art, 1987.

Wolf, Susan. "Theresa Cha: Recalling Telling Retelling," *Afterimage,* Summer 1986.

JIMMIE DURHAM

Born Washington, Arkansas, 1940
BFA, Ecole des Beaux Arts, University of Geneva, Switzerland, 1972

Selected Exhibitions and Performances

1992
Documenta 9, Kassel, Germany
*Nicole Klagsbrun Gallery, New York

1991
The Interrupted Life, New Museum of Contemporary Art, New York
Museum of Civilization, Hull, Quebec
*C.N. Gorman Gallery, University of California, Davis

1990
*Western Gallery, Western Washington University, Bellingham
The Decade Show, Museum of Contemporary Hispanic Art, The New Museum of Contemporary Art, and The Studio Museum of Harlem, New York (performance of *Crazy for Life,* Dance Theater Workshop, Whitney Museum of American Art, New York)
The Self-Taught Artist, Exit Art, New York (performance)
Savoir Faire, Savoir Vivre, Savoir Etre, Centre International d'Art Contemporain de Montréal, Quebec

1989
Jimmie Durham: The Bishop's Moose and the Pinkerton Men, Exit Art, New York (included performance, *Hermeneutical Considerations of the Bishop's Moose)*

1988
Re-Visions, Walter Phillips Gallery, Banff, Alberta
*Matt's Gallery, London, England
*Orchard Gallery, Derry, Northern Ireland

1987
We, The People, Artists' Space, New York (Co-curator)
Rider With No Horse, American Indian Gallery, New York
I Want To Say Something, La Mamma Theater, New York (performance)

1986
Ni'go tlunh a doh ka, State University of New York, Old Westbury, New York (Co-curator)
Por Encima El Bloqueo, Museum del Chopo, Mexico City; Centro Wifredo Lam, Havana, Cuba
Modern Anthropology, Bronx River Art Center, New York
Personal History, Public Address, Minor Injury Gallery, New York
Mixed Media, Mixed Mores, U.S. Courthouse, New York

1985
Alternative Museum, New York
Traditions and Modern Configurations, AAA Art, New York; Wake
Forest University, Winston-Salem

1984
Racist America, Dramatis Personae, New York

1983
Artists Call Against U.S. Intervention in Central America, Judson
Memorial Church, New York
Thanksgiving, P.S. 122, New York (performance)

Selected Bibliography

Canning, Susan. "Jimmie Durham," *Art Papers* 14/4 (1990).

Durham, Jimmie. "On the Edge of Town," *Art Journal,* Summer 1992.

_____. "Cowboys and...Notes on Art, Literature, and American Indians
in the Modern American Mind," in Annette Jaimes, ed. *The State of
Native America.* Boston: South End Press, 1992.

_____. "Jimmie Durham on Collecting," *Artforum,* May 1991.

_____. "The Immortal State," in *The Interrupted Life* (exhibition
catalog). New York: New Museum of Contemporary Art, 1991.

_____. "A Central Margin," in *The Decade Show: Frameworks of
Identity in the 1980s* (exhibition catalog). New York: Museum of
Contemporary Hispanic Art, The New Museum of Contemporary Art,
and the Studio Museum in Harlem, 1990.

_____. "The Ground Has Been Covered," *Artforum,* Summer 1988.

_____. "Those Dead Guys for a Hundred Years," in Brian Swann and
Arnold Hrupat, eds. *I Tell You Now.* Lincoln: University of Nebraska
Press, 1987.

_____. "Savage Attacks on White Women, as Usual," in *We, The People*
(exhibition catalog). New York: Artists Space, 1987.

_____. "Mr. Catlin and Mr. Rockefeller Tame the American Wilderness,"
in *An Anti-Catalogue.* New York: Artists for Cultural Change, 1976.

_____. "'Eloleh' ou le conseils de l'univers," in *Les Sept Points
Cardinaux: Orientations Eco-logiques.* Geneva: Institut Universitaire
d'Etudes du Developpement and Paris: Presses Universitaires de France.

Gleason, Judith. "Jimmie Durham," *Parnassus,* Fall 1984.

Ingberman, Jeanette, ed. *Jimmie Durham: The Bishop's Moose and the
Pinkerton Men* (exhibition catalog). New York: Exit Art, 1989.

Jones, Amelia. "Jimmie Durham: Exit Art," *Artscribe,* March 1990.

Lippard, Lucy R. *Mixed Blessings: New Art in a Multicultural America.*
New York: Pantheon, 1990.

_____. "Jimmie Durham," *The Guardian,* December 16, 1987.

Reid, Calvin. "Jimmie Durham: Exit Art," *Art in America,* May 1990.

Shiff, Richard. "The Necessity of Jimmie Durham's Jokes," *Art Journal,*
Fall 1992.

Smith, Roberta. "The Faces of Death," *New York Times,* September 13,
1991.

ANDY GOLDING

Born 1953
BA, Polytechnic of Central London, 1982

Selected Exhibitions

1992
Pure Land, multi-projector show with Alan Parker, Institute of
Contemporary Arts, London
1991
Public Images, Forum Stadtpark, Graz, Austria
Shocks to the System: Social and Political Issues in Recent British Art,
Royal Festival Hall, London
James Brown, slide show, The Milk Bar, Charing Cross Road, London

1989
Mysterious Coincidences, Photographers' Gallery, London
Nightmail VI, multi-projector installation, Club Quattro, Tokyo, Japan
Some Notions on Marginality, Grey Art Gallery, New York University

1988
Shifting Focus, Serpentine, London
The Other Body, Photographic Resource Center, Boston
Toward the Photograph as a Vulgar Document, Optica Gallery, Montreal
The Blues, Corner House, Manchester
Metro Billboard Project, Newcastle, Leeds, Derry, Manchester, Sheffield
Nightmail, multi-projector show with Alan Parker for *Time Out Live*
Exhibition, Olympia
Hidden Menace, collaboration with Jessica Evans, "The Mind,"
Impressions Gallery, New York

1987
The Body Politic, Photographers' Gallery, London

1985
Two New Towns, Cockpit Gallery, London

1984
Parents and Children, Harlow Playhouse, Harlow, Essex

1982
Poverty: The Unequal Struggle, New Conceptions, Cockpit Gallery, London

Selected Bibliography

Hevey, David. *The Creatures Time Forgot.* London: Routledge, 1992.

Rose, Cynthia. *Design After Dark.* London: Thames and Hudson, 1991.

Tabrizian, Mitra. *Correct Distance.* Manchester: Cornerhouse Publications,
1990.

GUILLERMO GOMEZ-PENA

Born Mexico City, 1955

Selected Exhibitions and Performances

1992
*The Year of the White Bear, Walker Art Center, Minneapolis

1990
The Decade Show, Museum of Contemporary Hispanic Art, The New
Museum of Contemporary Art, and The Studio Museum of Harlem, New
York

Selected Bibliography

Brookman, Philip. "Ocnoceni," *High Performance,* 8/2, 1985.
Carr, C. "Border Brujo," *Artforum,* January 1989.

Gómez-Peña, Guillermo. Statement in "On Nationality: Thirteen Artists,"
Art in America, September 1991.

_____. "From Art-maggedon to Gringo-stroika," *High Performance,* Fall
1991.

_____. "Death on the Border: A Eulogy to Border Art," *High Performance*, Spring 1991.

_____. "A New Artistic Document," in *Art in the Public Interest*. Ann Arbor: UMI Research Press, 1989.

_____. "The Multicultural Paradigm," *High Performance,* Fall 1989.

_____. "The Border Arts Workshop," with Coco Fusco, *Third Text,* Summer 1989.

_____. "Documented/Undocumented," in Rick Simonson and Scott Walker, eds. *The Graywolf Annual Five: Multi-Cultural Literary,* St. Paul, 1988.

_____. "Wacha es order, son," in *The Border Art Workshop/Taller de Arte Fronterizo: A Documentary of Five Years of Intedisciplinary Art Projects Dealing with U.S.-Mexico Issues: 1984–89.* San Diego: Border Art Workshop, 1988.

Hicks, Emily. "The Artist as Citizen," *High Performance,* 9/3, 1986.

Lippard, Lucy R. *Mixed Blessings: New Art in a Multicultural America.* New York: Pantheon, 1990.

Martin, Victoria. "Getting Unstuck from History," *Artweek,* October 4, 1990.

Mifflin, Margot. "Performance Art: What is it and where is it going?" *Art News,* April 1992.

Wei, Lilly, et al. "On Nationality: Thirteen Artists," *Art in America,* September 1991.

CONNIE HATCH

Born Muskogee, Oklahoma, 1951
BFA, University of Texas, Austin, 1973
MFA, San Francisco Art Institute, 1979

Selected Exhibitions, Performances

1992
Between a Rock and a Blind Spot, Roy Boyd Gallery, Santa Monica
We interrupt your regularly scheduled programming, White Columns, New York

1991
Sightlines, Newport Harbor Art Museum (installation for *Mapping Histories,* The Third Newport Biennial)

1990
After the Fact, Mills College Art Gallery, Oakland
Spectacular Women, Film in the Cities, St. Paul
Who Counts?, Randolph Street Gallery, Chicago

1989
Deliberate Investigations, Recent Works by Four Los Angeles Artists, Los Angeles County Museum of Art
Re-Presenting the Past, Capp Street Project, San Francisco
Confronting the Uncomfortable: Questioning Truth and Power, Yale University Art Gallery, New Haven
Camera Lucida, Walter Phillips Gallery, Banff, Alberta
After the Fact...Some Women, Roy Boyd Gallery, Santa Monica

1988
The BiNATIONAL: American Art of the Late 80s, Institute of Contemporary Art, Boston and Kunsthalle Dusseldorf, Germany
Photo-Generated, Roy Boyd Gallery, Santa Monica
L.A.C.E., Los Angeles
The DeSublimation of Romance, Light Work, Syracuse
Image and Text, Women's Building, Los Angeles

1987
Unavailability, New Langton Arts, San Francisco
Sexual Difference: Both Sides of the Camera, C.E.P.A., Buffalo; Columbia University, New York
Projections in Public, Bloomsbury City Flower Mart, Los Angeles (performance)

1986
Serving the Status Quo, New Museum of Contemporary Art, New York (performance trilogy)
There NOT Here, Here NOT There: The Exotic Image and Its Other, Nova Scotia College of Art and Design, Halifax

1985
The Nicaragua Media Project, Los Angeles Center for Photographic Studies
This Is Not About...Some Political Photographs of the 80s, Artemesia Gallery, Chicago

1984
Social Works, Banff Center for the Arts, Alberta, Canada
The Way We Live Now: Beyond Social Documentary, P.S.1, Long Island City, New York

1982
Form Follows Finance, Camerawork Gallery, San Francisco

Selected Bibliography

Carlson, Lance. "The Hermeneutics of Visual Fact," *Artweek,* August 12, 1989.

Durant, Mark. "Suspicious Secrets," *Artweek,* August 22, 1988.

Geer, Susan. "Hatch's Installation: Table for Two after Durer," *Los Angeles Times,* November 24, 1990.

Grover, Jan Zita. "Making Light," *Artweek,* October 25, 1986.

Hatch, Connie. "After the Fact," *Exposure,* Summer 1990.

_____. "Serving the Status-Quo," in Brian Wallis, ed. *Blasted Allegories: An Anthology of Writings by Contemporary Artists.* New York: New Museum of Contemporary Art, 1987.

_____. "The DeSublimation of Romance: Consider the Difference," in Sylvia Kolbowski, ed., *Wedge: Special Issue on Sexuality,* Winter 1984.

_____. "Form Follows Finance," *Obscura,* Summer 1983.

Joselit, David and Elisabeth Sussman. "Interview," in *American Art of the Late 80s: The BiNATIONAL.* Cologne: DuMont, 1988.

Kandel, Susan. "Dynamiting the Documentary," *Los Angeles Times,* April 20, 1992

Liss, Andrea. "Forced to Disappear," *Afterimage,* November 1989.

Penley, Constance. "The Artist, Politics, and the Image," in Renny Pritikin, ed. *Artists and Writers in Residence: 80 Langton Street.* San Francisco: 80 Langton Street, 1980.

Plagens, Peter. "Under Western Eyes," *Art in America,* January 1989.

Raczka, Robert. "Writing on the Wall," *Afterimage,* May 1988.

Rosler, Martha. "Some Contemporary Documentary," *Afterimage,* Summer 1983.

Solomon-Godeau, Abigail. *Sexual Difference: Both Sides of the Camera,* Minneapolis: University of Minnesota Press, 1991.

_____. "Reconstructing Documentary: Connie Hatch's Representational Resistance," *Camera Obscura,* Spring/Summer 1987.

_____. "Photography After Art Photography," in Brian Wallis, ed., *Art After Modernism*. New York: New Museum of Contemporary Art, 1984.

Welles, Elenore. "Society's Oppressive Weight," *Artweek*, July 9, 1988.

MARY KELLY

Born Minnesota, 1941
MA, Pius XII Institute, Florence, Italy, 1965
Postgraduate Diploma, St. Martin's School of Art, 1970

Selected Exhibitions

1991
Biennial Exhibition, Whitney Museum of American Art, New York
Gender and Representation, Zoller Gallery, Pennsylvania State University

1990
*Interim. New Museum of Contemporary Art, New York
Word as Image, Milwaukee Art Museum; Museum of Contemporary Art, Houston
The Decade Show, Museum of Contemporary Hispanic Art, The New Museum of Contemporary Art, The Studio Museum in Harlem, New York

1989
*Postmasters Gallery, New York
*C.E.P.A., Buffalo, NY

1988
*McNeil Gallery, Philadelphia
*L.A.C.E., Los Angeles
*Galerie Powerhouse, Montreal
Modes of Address, Whitney Museum of American Art Downtown, New York

1987
Conceptual Clothing, Ikon Gallery, Birmingham, England
State of the Art, Institute of Contemporary Art, London, England

1986
*A Space, Toronto
*Kettles Yard, Cambridge University
Identity/Desire: Representing the Body, Collins Gallery, University of Strathclyde, Glasgow

1985
*Fruitmarket Gallery, Edinburgh
Difference: Representation and Sexuality, The New Museum of Contemporary Art, New York

1984
The Critical Eye/I, Yale Center for British Art, New Haven

1983
The Revolutionary Power of Woman's Laughter, Max Protetch Gallery, New York

1982
*George Paton Gallery, Melbourne, Australia
*University Art Museum, Brisbane, Australia
4th Biennale of Sydney, Gallery of New South Wales

Selected Bibliography

Bryson, Norman, Griselda Pollock, Gary Sangster, Marcia Tucker, Hal Foster. *Mary Kelly—Interim.* New York: New Museum of Contemporary Art, 1990.

Cottingham, Laura. "Thoughts are Things; What is a Woman?," *Contemporanea*, September 1990.

Fisher, Jennifer. "Interview with Mary Kelly," *Parachute,* July–September, 1989.

Foster, Hal. "The Future of an Illusion," *Endgame* (exhibition catalog), Boston: Institute of Contemporary Art, 1987.

Gott, Richard. "Interim Reflections," *The Guardian,* June 2, 1986.

Iverson, Margaret. "Fashioning Feminine Identity," *Art International,* Spring 1988.

_____. "Difference: On Representation and Sexuality," *m/f* 11&12 (1986).

Mary Kelly. "On 'Interim,' Part I," *WhiteWalls,* Fall 1989.

_____. "On Difference, Sexuality and Sameness," *Screen* 28/1 (1987).

_____. "Invisible Bodies: On Interim," *New Formations* 2 (1987).

_____. "Interim," *The Guardian,* June 2,9,16,23,30, 1986.

_____. "Mary Kelly in Conversation with Laura Mulvey," *Afterimage,* March 1986.

_____. "Menacé," *Talking Back to the Media*, Amsterdam, 1985.

_____. "Reviewing Modernist Criticism," in Brian Wallis, ed., *Art After Modernism: Rethinking Representation,* New York: New Museum of Contemporary Art, 1984.

_____. *Post-Partum Document.* London: Routledge & Kegan Paul, 1983.

Mulvey, Laura. "Impending Time," in *Interim*. Edinburgh: Fruitmarket Gallery, 1985.

Paoletti, John. "Mary Kelly's Interim," *Arts*, October 1985.

Pollock, Griselda. *Vision and Difference: Femininity, Feminism and Histories of Art.* London, New York: Routledge & Kegan Paul, 1988.

Rehberg, Andrea. "The Deconstructing Difference Issue of Screen," *Independent Media*, May 1987.

Shottenkirk, Dena. "Mary Kelly," *Artforum,* May 1990.

Watney, Simon. "Mary Kelly," *Artscribe,* March/April 1987.

Wintman, Elaine. "In the Interim," *Articles* 4/1 (1988).

GLENN LIGON

Born Bronx, New York, 1960
BA, Wesleyan University, Middletown, Connecticut, 1982
Whitney Museum Independent Study Program, 1985

Selected Exhibitions

1992
*Max Protetch Gallery, New York
Contemporary Drawing: Allegories of Modernism, Museum of Modern Art, New York
Knowledge: Aspects of Conceptual Art, University Art Museum, Santa Barbara

1991
*White Columns, New York
Biennial Exhibition, Whitney Museum of American Art, New York
Interrogating Identity, Grey Art Gallery, New York
Positions of Authority, Art in General, New York
Text Out of Context, Soho Center, New York

1990
*Winter Exhibition Series, P.S.1, New York
*How It Feels to be Colored Me, BACA Downtown, Brooklyn
Spent: Currency, Security and Art on Deposit, New Museum of
Contemporary Art at Marine Midland Bank, New York
Works on Paper, Selena Art Gallery, Long Island University, Brooklyn
Art of Resistance, El Bohio, New York
Public Mirror, Art Against Racism, Clocktower Gallery, New York

1989
Selections 46, The Drawing Center, New York

Selected Bibliography

Colpitt, Frances and Phyllis Plous. Knowledge: Aspects of Conceptual
Art (exhibition catalog). Santa Barbara: University Art Museum, 1992.

Faust, Gretchen. "New York in Review," Arts, December 1990.

Harris, Patty. "Artists and Minority Identity," Downtown, May 29,
1991.

Larson, Kay. "A Sock to the System," New York Magazine, April 26,
1991.

Ligon, Glenn. "Insert," artist pages for Parkett, December 1991.

_____. "Profiles," artist pages for Third Text, Summer 1991.

Nesbitt, Lois E. "Interrogating Identity," Artforum, Summer 1991.

Smith, Roberta. "'Lack of Location is My Location'," New York Times,
June 16, 1991.

Temin, Christine. "The Art of Questioning Identity," Boston Globe,
August 4, 1991.

_____. "'Interrogating Identity': The View from the Outside," The
Boston Globe, August 13, 1991.

YONG SOON MIN

Born South Korea, 1953
BA, University of California, Berkeley, 1975
MA, University of California, Berkeley, 1977
MFA, University of California, Berkeley, 1979
Whitney Museum Independent Study Program, 1981

Selected Exhibitions

1991
*Bronx Museum of the Arts, New York
Maps and Madness, Marine Midland Bank/Soho, New York
Howard Yezerski Gallery, Boston
Rockland Center for the Arts, New York

1990
Disputed Identities, UK/US, San Francisco Camerawork
The Decade Show, Museum of Contemporary Hispanic Art,
The New Museum of Contemporary Art, The Studio Museum
in Harlem, New York
Art Against Apartheid, Jamaica Art Center, New York
Occupation and Resistance: American Impressions of the Intifada,
Alternative Museum, New York
Signs of Self: Changing Perceptions, Woodstock Artists Association,
New York
Art in the Anchorage, Creative Time, Brooklyn, NY

1989
Land and the Elements, Luise Ross Gallery, New York
Literacy on the Table — Cultural Fluency and the Act of Reading,
Franklin Furnace, New York
Beyond Survival: Old Frontiers, New Visions, Ceres Gallery, New York

1988
Selections from the Artists File, Artists Space, New York
Autobiography: In Her Own Image, INTAR Gallery, New York
Committed to Print, Museum of Modern Art, New York

1987
Up South, BACA Downtown Gallery, New York
Jamaica Art Center, New York

1986
Soho 20 Gallery, New York

1985
Roots to Reality, Henry Street Settlement Gallery, New York
Stifel Fine Arts Center, Oglebay Institute, West Virginia

1984
*Ohio University Gallery

1983
Ohio Selections II, Gallery of Contemporary Art, Cleveland

1982
Arsenal Annex Gallery, New York
Athens International Film & Video Festival, Athens, Ohio

Selected Bibliography

Contemporary Art by Women of Color. The Guadalupe Cultural Arts
Center, 1990.

Langer, Cassandra. Positions, Reflections on Multi-racial Issues in the
Visual Arts. New York Feminist Art Institute, 1990.

Leval, Susana. Signs of the Self: Changing Perceptions (exhibition catalog).
New York: Woodstock Artists Association, 1990.

Lippard, Lucy R. Mixed Blessings: New Art in a Multicultural America.
New York: Pantheon, 1990.

Machida, Margo. "Seeing Yellow," in The Decade Show: Frameworks of
Identity in the 1980s (exhibition catalog). New York: Museum of
Contemporary Hispanic Art, The New Museum of Contemporary Art, and
the Studio Museum in Harlem, 1990.

Reid, Calvin. "Inside/Outside," Art in America, 1991.

Roth, Moira. Autobiography: In Her Own Image. New York: INTAR
Gallery, 1988.

Smith, Roberta. "In a Show on the Issues, the Focus is Outrage," New York
Times, 1990.

Smith, Valerie. Selections from the Artists File. New York: Artists Space,
1988.

Yong Soon Min. "Comparing the Contemporary Experiences of Asian
American, South Korean and Cuban Artists," in Shirley Hune, et. al., eds.
Asian Americans: Comparative and Global Perspectives. Washington State
University Press, 1991.

_____. "Our World Within," in Ancestors Known and Unknown -
Boxworks (exhibition catalog). Coast to Coast, National Women Artists of
Color, 1991.

_____. "Territorial Waters: Mapping Asian American Cultural Identity,"
Harbour, Magazine of Art and Everyday Life, 1990.

_____. "Min Joong," Art and Artists, 1987.

ADRIAN PIPER

Born New York City, 1948
AA, School of Visual Arts, New York, 1969
BA, Philosophy, City College of New York, 1974
MA, Philosophy, Harvard University, 1977
PhD, Philosophy, Harvard University, 1981

Selected Exhibitions, Performances

1992
*Political Drawings and Installations, 1975–1991, Cleveland Center for Contemporary Art
Dispossessed Installations, Florida State University, Tallahassee
1991
*Adrian Piper: European Retrospective, Ikon Gallery, Birmingham, England
*What It's Like, What It Is #1, Washington Project for the Arts, Washington, DC
*Directions: What It's Like, What It Is #2, Hirshhorn Museum, Washington, DC
Dislocations, Museum of Modern Art, New York [installation of What It's Like, What It Is #3]
Gender and Representation, Zoller Gallery, Pennsylvania State University
The Art of Advocacy, Aldrich Museum of Contemporary Art, Ridgefield
Artists of Conscience: 16 Years of Social and Political Commentary, Alternative Museum, New York

1990
*Why Guess?, University of Rhode Island Art Gallery, Kingston
*Out of the Corner, Whitney Museum of American Art, Film and Video Gallery, New York
Signs of the Self: Changing Perceptions, Woodstock Artists Association, New York
Word as Image: American Art 1960–1990, Milwaukee Art Museum
Presumed Identities, Real Art Ways, Hartford
*Williams College Art Museum, Williamstown, MA

1989
*John Weber Gallery, New York
*Matrix Gallery, University Art Museum, Berkeley
Making Their Mark: Women Artists Move Into the Mainstream 1970–85, Cincinnati Art Museum
Buttinsky, Feature Gallery, New York
I Only Want You to Love Me, Feature Gallery, New York

1988
Autobiography: In Her Own Image, INTAR Gallery, New York
Committed to Print, Museum of Modern Art, New York

1987
*Adrian Piper: Reflections 1967–1987, Alternative Museum, New York
Black Video: Performance/Document/Narrative, C.N. Gorman Gallery, University of California, Davis

1986
*My Calling (Card) #1, Dinner/Cocktail Party Reactive Guerrilla Performance
*My Calling (Card) #2, Disco/Bar Reactive Guerrilla Performance

1985
Tradition and Conflict, Studio Museum in Harlem, New York
Kunst mit Eigen-Sinn, Museum Moderner Kunst, Vienna
The Art of Memory/The Loss of History, The New Museum of Contemporary Art, New York

1983
The Black and White Show, Kenkeleba Gallery, New York
Language, Drama, Source and Vision, The New Museum of Contemporary Art, New York
*Funk Lessons, various sites (performance)

Selected Bibliography

Adrian Piper: Reflections 1967–1987 (exhibition catalog). New York: Alternative Museum, 1987.

Als, Hilton. "Spotlight: Adrian Piper," Flash Art, Summer 1989.

Barrie, Lita. "Shedding her Male Identity," Artweek, March 14, 1991.

Berger, Maurice. "The Critique of Pure Racism: An Interview with Adrian Piper," Afterimage, October 1990.

Brenson, Michael. "Adrian Piper's Head-On Confrontation of Racism," The New York Times, October 26, 1990.

Coleman, Wanda. "A Second Heart: Racism, Identity, and the Blues Aesthetic," High Performance, Winter 1990.

Danto, Arthur. "Dislocationary Art," The Nation, January 6, 1992.

Hayt-Atkins, Elizabeth. "The Indexical Present: A Conversation with Adrian Piper," Arts Magazine, March 1991.

Knight, Christopher. "Looking Racism in the Face," Los Angeles Times, March 5, 1991.

Kuspit, Donald. "Art and the Moral Imperative," New Art Examiner, January 1991.

Lippard, Lucy R. Mixed Blessings: New Art in a Multicultural America. New York: Pantheon, 1990.

_____. Get the Message? A Decade of Art for Social Change. New York: E.P. Dutton, 1984.

_____. From the Center: Feminist Essays on Women's Art. New York: E.P. Dutton, 1976.

McEvilley, Thomas. "Adrian Piper," Artforum, September 1987.

Olander, William. "Fragments," in The Art of Memory/The Loss of History (exhibition catalog). New York: New Museum of Contemporary Art, 1985.

Piper, Adrian. I Am Not a Token, I Am Not a Type. Video and Audio-Box, with critical essays by Lawrence Alloway, Claudia Barrow, Maurice Berger, and Lucy Lippard. Seattle: University of Washington Press, (forthcoming).

_____. "My Calling (Cards) #1 and #2," Harper's Magazine (forthcoming).

_____. "Cornered: A Video Installation Project by Adrian Piper," Movement Research Performance Journal, Winter/Spring 1992.

_____. Colored People. London: Bookworks, 1991.

_____. "The Joy of Marginality," Art Papers, July–August 1990.

_____. "The Triple Negation of Colored Women Artists," Next Generation Catalogue. Chapel Hill: University of North Carolina, 1990.

_____. "Xenophobia and the Indexical Present," and "Funk Lessons," in Mark O'Brien, ed. Re-Imaging America: The Arts of Social Change. Philadelphia: New Society Press, 1990.

_____. "Cornered," Balcon 4 (1989).

_____. "Who Is Safely White," Women Artists News, June 1987.

_____. Untitled Statement. The Art of Memory/The Loss of History (exhibition catalog). New York: New Museum of Contemporary Art, 1985.

_____. "Ideology, Confrontation, and Political Self-Awareness: An Essay," High Performance, Spring 1981.
Rinder, Lawrence. "Adrian Piper: Racism Confronted," MATRIX/Berkeley 130 (exhibition brochure). Berkeley: University Art Museum, August 1989.

Roth, Moira, ed. The Amazing Decade: Women and Performance in America, 1970–1980. Los Angeles, Astro Artz, 1983.

Storr, Robert. Dislocations (exhibition catalog). New York: Museum of Modern Art, 1991.

Welish, Marjorie. "In This Corner, Adrian Piper's Agitprop," *Arts Magazine*, March 1991.

Wilson, Judith. "'In Memory of the News and of Ourselves': The Art of Adrian Piper," *Third Text*, Autumn/Winter 1991.

ARMANDO RASCON

Born Calexico, California, 1956
BA, Fine Arts, College of Creative Studies, University of California, Santa Barbara, 1979

Selected Exhibitions

1992
Existential Monochrome, Randolph Street Gallery, Chicago
Tales of Desire, Artists Space, New York
Multiplicity, Robbin Lockett Gallery, Chicago
Information Culture Technology, San Francisco State University

1991
Two Projects: The Black Museum and The Multicultural Reading Room (with Danny Tisdale), Randolph Street Gallery, Chicago
1992: Conquests Do Not Belong Only to the Past, Projections Project, INTAR Gallery, New York
Beyond 1992: Experiments in Cross-Cultural Collaboration, various sites, Toronto, Canada
Burning in Hell, Franklin Furnace, New York
S & L: Transactions in the Post-industrial Era, Walter/McBean Gallery, San Francisco Art Institute
The Human Mark, Center for the Arts, Yerba Buena Gardens, San Francisco

1990
The Multicultural Reading Room: Center for Research and Information, New Langton Arts, San Francisco
Body/Culture: Chicano Figuration, Sonoma State University
Dia de Los Muertos, Alternative Museum, New York

1989
The AIDS Timeline [Group Material installation], MATRIX Gallery, University Art Museum, Berkeley
Dia de Los Muertos: Los Angelitos, Alternative Museum, New York

1988
Mano a Mano, University of California, Santa Cruz, and the Art Museum of Santa Cruz County

1987
Corporate Crime/Malicious Mischief, INSTALLATION Gallery, San Diego
Vertigo: The Poetics of Dislocation, San Francisco Art Institute
Mexican/American Art, Salon de Actos de la Loteria Nacional, Mexico City

1986
Art After Eden: An Unnatural Perspective, Southern Exposure Gallery, San Francisco

1985
Chain Reaction, San Francisco Arts Commission Gallery

1984
Temple of the Assassins (performance with Irwin Irwin), New Langton Arts, San Francisco

1983
The Impolite Figure, Southern Exposure Gallery and Bannam Place Exhibition Place, San Francisco

1982
Water, Water, Galeria Picasso, Santa Barbara

Selected Bibliography

Bonetti, David. "At alternative spaces, the business of art is politics," *San Francisco Examiner,* September 26, 1991.

Bowen, Cathleen. "Art and Politics," *VOX Magazine,* Winter 1990.

Friedman, Robert. "Caught in the Capitalist NEXUS," *San Francisco Sentinel,* September 12, 1991.

Jenkins, Steven. "Conversation with Armando Rascon," *Artweek* 32/31, 1991.

Matthews, Lydia. "Armando Rascon at Southern Exposure Gallery," *VISIONS Art Quarterly,* Spring 1992.

Rascón, Armando. "Re-interpreting Miss Rucker's American History Lesson, Fifth Grade, Jefferson Elementary, Calexico, California, School Term 1966-67," in Roberto Bedoya and Karen Atkinson, eds., "Rediscovery," *Frame/Work* 5/1 (1992).

_____. "Pendant Bell with Eagle Warrior," in Karen Atkinson, ed., "New World Women 1992," *New Observations,* Winter 1992.

_____. "The Multicultural Reading Room: Center for Research and Information," in Maureen Sherlock, ed., "Bifocal Borders," *Art Papers,* 1992.

_____. "Untitled (Quincentennial Recipe)," in Robin Kahn, ed., *S.O.S. Int'l,* Winter 1992.

MARLON RIGGS

Select Filmography

1992
Non, Je ne Regrette Rien

1991
Anthem
Color Adjustment
Circle of Recovery

1990
Affirmations

1989
Visions Toward Tomorrow: Ida Louise Jackson
Tongues Untied

1988
Open Window: Innovations from the University of California

1987
Ethnic Notions
Changing Images: Mirrors of Life, Molds of Reality

1982
Long Train Running: The Story of the Oakland Blues

Selected Bibliography

Anwar, Farrah. "Tongues Untied," *Sight & Sound,* July 1991.

Berger, Maurice. "Art and Politics II: Too Shocking to Show?" *Art in America,* July 1992.

Cripps, Thomas. "Ethnic notions," *Cineaste,* 17/1, 1989.

Fox, Nichols. "PBS Tongue Tied on Gay Issues," *New Art Examiner,* October 1991.

Goodeve, Thyrza. "Tongues Untied," *Cineaste,* 18/1, 1990.

Harris, Lyle Ashton. "Cultural Healing," *Afterimage,* March 1991.

Riggs, Marlon. "Notes of a signifyin' snap! Queen," *Art Journal,* Fall 1991.

Risatti, Howard. "Editorials: Richmond, Va.," *New Art Examiner,* October 1991.

Sims, Lowery. "Two snaps up for Marlon Riggs," *High Performance,* Fall 1990.

Soe, Valerie. "Recollections of the Human Experience," *Artweek,* March 1, 1990.

MARTHA ROSLER

Born New York City, 1942
BA, Brooklyn College of the City University of New York, 1965
MFA, University of California, San Diego, 1974

Selected Exhibitions, Performances

1992
Green Acres: Neo-Colonialism in the U.S., Washington University Gallery of Art, St. Louis [installation of *If You Lived Here: Homelessness and Housing in St. Louis]*
Empowering the Viewer: Art, Politics, and the Community, William Benton Museum of Art, University of Connecticut
Dirt and Domesticity: Constructions of the Feminine, Whitney Museum of American Art
Video: Two Decades, Museum of Modern Art, New York

1991
The Family Show, Artists Space, New York
*S&L: Transactions in the Post-Industrial Era, San Francisco Art Institute
*(Dis)Membered, Simon Watson, New York
Artists of Conscience: 16 Years of Social and Political Commentary, Alternative Museum
Woman as Subject: From the Surface to the Core, The Kitchen, New York

1990
The Power of Words: An Aspect of Recent Documentary Photography, P.P.O.W. Gallery, New York
Crossing Boundaries in Feminist History, Douglass College, New Brunswick
Four Photo Feminisms, Rutgers Summerfest Exhibit, New Brunswick
The Decade Show, Museum of Contemporary Hispanic Art, The New Museum of Contemporary Art, The Studio Museum in Harlem, New York
Video and Myth, Museum of Modern Art, New York
Housing is a Human Right, Museum of Modern Art, Oxford

1989
Making Their Mark: Women Artists 1970-1985, Cincinnati Art Museum
Mediated Issues: Women, Myth, & Sexuality, Institute of Contemporary Art, Boston
Prisoners of Image, 1800-1988: Ethnic and Gender Stereotypes, Alternative Museum, New York

1988
*Martha Rosler: Four Works, Long Beach Museum of Art
Talking Terrorism: Ideologies and Paradigms in a Postmodern World, Stanford University Humanities Center
The Third Wave: International Women's Film and Video Festival, Liatris Media, Austin, Texas
Unacceptable Appetites, Artists Space, New York
That's Progress, Los Angeles Center for Photographic Studies
*Born to Be Sold: Martha Rosler Reads the Strange Case of Baby $M, American Film Institute Video Festival, Los Angeles

1987
*Focus: Martha Rosler, Institute of Contemporary Art, Boston
Global Taste: A Meal in Three Courses, Cornell Cinema, Ithaca
Sexual Difference: Both Sides of the Camera, C.E.P.A., Buffalo; Columbia University, New York
Biennial Exhibition, Whitney Museum of American Art, New York
Social Engagement: Women's Video in the '80s, Whitney Museum of American Art, New York

1986
Mass: A Group Material Project, New Museum of Contemporary Art, New York
National Video Festival, American Film Institute, Chicago
In the Tradition of...Photography, Light Gallery, New York
Electronic Arts Gallery, Minneapolis

1985
Against the Conventional Definitions of Sexuality, Articule Gallery, Montreal
What Does She Want?, Artists Space, New York
The Art of Memory, The Loss of History, New Museum of Contemporary Art, New York
Disinformation: The Manufacture of Consent, Alternative Museum, New York
Brennpunkt: Kunst mit Eigen-Sinn, Museum Moderner Kunst, Vienna

1984
Difference: On Representation and Sexuality, New Museum of Contemporary Art, New York
Public Affairs, AKA Propaganda, Franklin Furnace, New York
Politics in Art, Queensborough Community College, New York
Street Culture: A Video Series, Video Inn, Vancouver

1983
*Martha Rosler: Six Videotapes, 1975–1983, The Office, New York
Roles, Relationships, Sexuality, Long Beach Museum of Art
Mediated Narratives, Institute of Contemporary Art, Boston
Video Art: A History, Part II, Museum of Modern Art, New York

1982
Sense and Sensibility, Midlands Group, Nottingham, England
Redirection, Dance Theatre Workshop, New York
Text/Picture Notes, Visual Studies Workshop, Rochester
Mixing Art and Politics, Randolph Street Gallery, New York
Video by Women, The Kitchen, New York

Selected Bibliography

Buchloh, Benjamin H.D., "Documenta 7," *October,* Fall 1982.

Fichter, Robert and Paul Rutkovsky. "Interview with Martha Rosler," *Art Papers,* January/February 1988.

Hutcheon, Linda. "Fringe Interference: Postmodern Border Tensions," *Style,* Summer 1988.

Larsen, Ernest. "Who Owns the Streets?," *Art in America,* January 1990.

Lippard, Lucy. *Get the Message? A Decade of Art for Social Change.* New York: E.P. Dutton, 1984.

McGee, Micki. "Narcissism, Feminism, and Video Art: Some Solutions to a Problem of Representation," *Heresies,* 1981.

Olander, William. "Women and the Media: A Decade of New Video," in Patty Podesta, ed. *Resolution: A Critique of Video Art.* Los Angeles. L.A.C.E., 1986.

_____. "Fragments," in *The Art of Memory, The Loss of History* (exhibition catalog). New York: New Museum of Contemporary Art, 1983.

Owens, Craig. "Martha Rosler," *Profile,* Spring 1986.

_____. "The Discourse of Others: Feminism and Postmodernism," in Hal Foster, ed. *The Anti-Aesthetic: Essays on Postmodernism and Culture.* Seattle: Bay Press, 1983.

Parker, Roszika and Griselda Pollock. *Framing Feminism: Art and the Women's Movement*. London and New York: Methuen, 1987.

Rosler, Martha. "In, Around, and Afterthoughts: On Documentary Photography," in Richard Bolton, ed. *The Contest of Meaning: Critical Histories of Photography*. Cambridge: MIT Press, 1990.

_____. "Constructing a Life," in Brian Wallis, ed. *Blasted Allegories: An Anthology of Writings by Contemporary Artists*. New York: New Museum of Contemporary Art, 1987.

_____. "The Birth and Death of the Viewer: On the Public Function of Art," in Hal Foster, ed. *Art and the Public Sphere*. Seattle: Bay Press, 1987.

Roth, Moira, ed., *The Amazing Decade: Women and Performance Art in America, 1970-1980*. Los Angeles: Astro Artz, 1983.

Sayre, Henry. *The Object of Performance*. Chicago: University of Chicago Press, 1989.

Solomon-Godeau, Abigail. *Sexual Difference: Both Sides of the Camera*, Minneapolis: University of Minnesota Press, 1991.

_____. "Photography After Art Photography," in Brian Wallis, ed. *Art After Modernism: Rethinking Representation*, New York: New Museum of Contemporary Art, 1984.

LORNA SIMPSON

Born Brooklyn, New York, 1960
BFA, School of Visual Arts, New York, 1982
MFA, University of California, San Diego, 1985

Selected Exhibitions

1992
*Temple Gallery, Tyler School of Art, Philadelphia
*Josh Baer Gallery, New York
*Lorna Simpson: For the Sake of the Viewer, Museum of Contemporary Art, Chicago
Selected Works by African American Artists, Philadelphia Museum of Art
Dirt and Domesticity: Constructions of the Feminine, Whitney Museum of American Art
Dream Singers, Story Tellers: An African-American Presence, Fukai Fine Arts Museum, Fukai City, Japan
*Rhona Hoffman Gallery, Chicago
*Ansel Adams Center, San Francisco

1991
Constructed Images: New Photography, The Studio Museum in Harlem, New York
*C.E.P.A., Buffalo
de-Persona, Oakland Museum
*Gallery of the Department of Art and Art History, Dana Arts Center, Colgate University, Hamilton, NY
Biennial Exhibition, Whitney Museum of American Art, New York
Speak, Randolph Street Gallery, Chicago
Swartze Kunst: Konzepte zur Politik und Identität, Neue Gesellschaft für Bildende Kunst, Berlin
Artists of Conscience: Sixteen Years of Social and Political Commentary, Alternative Museum, New York
Devil on the Stairs: Looking Back on the '80s, Institute of Contemporary Art, University of Pennsylvania, Philadelphia

1990
Lorna Simpson: Recent Phototexts, 1989–1990, Denver Art Museum
Lorna Simpson: Projects 23, Museum of Modern Art, New York
Centric 38: Lorna Simpson, University Art Museum, California State University, Long Beach
Constructive Anger, Barbara Krakow Gallery, Boston

The Decade Show, Museum of Contemporary Hispanic Art, The New Museum of Contemporary Art, The Studio Museum in Harlem, New York
Awards in the Visual Arts 9, New Orleans Museum of Art

1989
Beyond Family of Man, Northeastern University Art Gallery, Boston
The Cutting Edge, Fine Arts Museum of Long Island, New York
Constructed Images: New Photography, Studio Museum of Harlem
Prisoners of Image 1800–1988: Ethnic and Gender Stereotypes, Alternative Museum, New York
*Matrix, Wadsworth Atheneum, Hartford, CT

1988
Autobiography: In Her Own Image, INTAR Gallery, New York
Politics of Gender, Queensboro College City University, Queens
Female (Re)Production, White Columns, New York
Utopia Post Utopia, Institute of Contemporary Art, Boston
*Jamaica Arts Center, Queens, NY
*Mercer Union, Toronto
The BiNATIONAL: American Art of the Late 80s, Institute of Contemporary Art, Boston and Kunsthalle Dusseldorf, Germany

1987
Documenta 8, Kassel, Germany
Deca-Dance, New Museum of Contemporary Art, New York

1986
The Body, New Museum of Contemporary Art, New York
Reflections on Self: Woman Photographers, Lowenstein Library Gallery, Fordham University, New York
America: Another Perspective, Photo Center Gallery, New York University
*Screens, Just Above Midtown Gallery, New York

1985
Seeing is Believing, Alternative Museum, New York
*Gestures/Reenactments, 5th Street Market Alternative Gallery, San Diego

1984
Contemporary Afro-American Photography, Allen Memorial Art Museum, Oberlin College

1983
Our Point of View, William Grant Still Community Center, Los Angeles
Dropped Lines, Seneca Falls Gallery, San Diego

1982
Heresies Annual Show, Frank Marino Gallery, New York
Working Women/Working Artists/Working Together, Bread and Roses Cultural Project, Inc. District 1199, New York

Selected Bibliography

Boyd, Blanche McCrary. "Spoleto U.S.A.," *Arts Magazine*, October 1991.

Collins, Bradford R. "History Lessons," *Art in America*, November 1991.

Faust, Gretchen. "Lorna Simpson," *Arts Magazine*, September 1991.

Fusco, Coco, "Uncanny Dissonances: The Work of Lorna Simpson," in *Lorna Simpson* (exhibition catalog). Hamilton, NY: The Gallery of the Department of Art History, Dana Arts Center, Colgate University, 1991.

Garfield, Donald. "This Exhibit Translates the Visual Vocabulary of Power," *Museum News*, September/October 1991.

Jones, Kellie. "In Their Own Image," *Artforum*, November 1990.

Joseph, Regina. "Interview with Lorna Simpson," *Balcon 5–6* (1990).

Koether, Jutta. "Lorna Simpson: Psychosoziale Forschungen," *Artis*, December/January 1991.

Lippard, Lucy R. *Mixed Blessings: New Art in a Multicultural America*. New York: Pantheon, 1990.

Malen, Lenore. "The Real Politics of Lorna Simpson," *Women Artists News* 13/3 (1988).

McKenna, Kristine. "Centric 38: High-Minded World of New York's Lorna Simpson," *Los Angeles Times,* April 3, 1990.

Plagens, Peter. "Under Western Eyes," *Art in America,* January 1989.

Sims, Lowery Stokes. "The Mirror, The Other: The Politics of Esthetics," *Artforum,* March 1990.

Smith, Roberta. "Working the Gap Between Art and Politics," *The New York Times,* September 25, 1988.

Trend, David. "The Object and Subject of Black Photography," *Afterimage,* May 1986.

Wallach, Amei. "Lorna Simpson: Right Time, Right Place," *New York Newsday,* September 19, 1990.

Wallis, Brian. "Questioning Documentary," *Aperture,* Fall 1988.

Zaya, Octavio. "Towards a Reconsideration of the Artistic Practice? (Art and Politics in the United States)," *Balcon* 8–9 (1992).

MITRA TABRIZIAN

Born Tehran, Iran, 1954
BA, Polytechnic of Central London, 1979
MPhil, Polytechnic of Central London, 1983

Selected Exhibitions

1992
History Present, Museum Folkwang, Essen, Germany
Fine Material for a Dream...? A Reappraisal of Orientalism: 19th & 20th Century Fine Art & Popular Culture, Harris Museum, Preston, England

1991
Shocks to the System: Social and Political Issues in Recent British Art, Royal Festival Hall, London
Public Images, Forum Stadtpark, Graz, Austria

1990
Spectacular Women, Film in the Cities Gallery, St. Paul
Contemporary Social Documentary, Fotobienal, Art History Center, Vigo, Spain

1989
Mysterious Coincidences, Photographers' Gallery, London
Shifting Focus, Serpentine Gallery, London
Through the Looking Glass: Photographic Art in Britain, 1945–1989, Barbican Art Gallery, London

1988
The Other Body, Photographic Resource Center, Boston
*The Actress, Portfolio Gallery, Edinburgh
Toward the Photograph as a Vulgar Document, Optica Gallery, Montreal
Sexual Difference: Both Sides of the Camera, Wallach Art Gallery, Columbia University, New York
*The Blues, Corner House, Manchester

1987
The Body Politic, Photographers' Gallery, London
Governmentality, Impressions Gallery, York

1986
Correct Distance, Photographers' Gallery, London
International Photography, Arles International Gallery, Arles, France

1985
Magnificent Obsession, ARC Gallery, Toronto
Impostors, Perspectief, Rotterdam, Holland
Towards a Bigger Picture, Victoria and Albert Museum, London

1984
College of Fashion, Gallery 400, Chicago
European Women Photographers Today, Torino Fotografia, Turin, Italy

1983
Beyond the Purloined Image, The Riverside Gallery, London
The Way We Live Now: Beyond Social Documentary, P.S.1, Long Island City, Queens, New York

1982
Phototextes, Musée d'Art et d'Histoire, Geneva
Light Reading, B2 Gallery, London

Selected Bibliography

Bright, Deborah. "The Other Body of British Photography," *Afterimage,* November 1987.

Jones, Kellie. "In Their Own Image," *Artforum,* November 1990.

Lee, David. "Photography," *Arts Review,* June 28, 1991.

Mulvey, Laura. *Visual and Other Pleasures.* Bloomington: Indiana University Press, 1989.

Pollock, Griselda. *Vision and Difference: Femininity, Feminism and Histories of Art.* London, New York: Routledge & Kegan Paul, 1988.

Tabrizian, Mitra. *Correct Distance.* Manchester: Cornerhouse Publications, 1990.

_____. "Correct Distance," *Creative Camera,* April 1986.

Tarentino, Michael. "The Other Body," *Artforum,* February 1988.

Tawadros, Gilane. "Other Britains, other Britons," *Aperture,* Winter 1988.

CARRIE MAE WEEMS

Born Portland, Oregon, 1953
BA, California Institute of the Arts, Valencia, 1981
MFA, University of California, San Diego, 1984
Graduate Program in Folklore, University of California, Berkeley, 1984–87

Selected Exhibitions

1992
*P.P.O.W. Gallery, New York
Schwarze Kunst: Konzepte zur Politik und Identität, Neue Gesellschaft für Bildende Kunst, Berlin
Pleasures and Terrors of Domestic Comfort, Museum of Modern Art, New York
Art, Politics and Community, William Benton Museum of Art, University of Connecticut, Storrs
Disclosing the Myth of the Family, Betty Rymer Gallery, School of the Art Institute of Chicago

1991
*Institute of Contemporary Art, Boston
*And 22 Million Very Tired and Very Angry People, New Museum of Contemporary Art, New York
Biennial Exhibition, Whitney Museum of American Art, New York
*Matrix 115, Wadsworth Atheneum, Hartford, CT
Sexuality, Image and Control, Houston Center for Photography
Disputed Identities, California Museum of Photography, Riverside

1990
Who Counts?, Randolph Street Gallery, Chicago
Signs of Self: Changing Perceptions, Woodstock Artists Association, Woodstock, NY
Cultural Diversity, Southern Illinois University, Carbondale
Presumed Identities, Real Art Ways, Hartford
Calling Out My Name, C.E.P.A., Buffalo, NY

1989
Self Portrayals, University Art Museum, State University of New York, Binghamton
A Century of Protest, Williams College, Williamstown, MA
*Rhode Island School of Design, Providence

1988
Herstory; Black Women Photographers, Firehouse Gallery, Houston
Prisoners of Image, 1800–1988, Alternative Museum, New York

1987
Visible Differences, Centro Cultural de la Raza, San Diego
Documenta 8, Kassel, Germany

1986
Social Concerns, Maryland Institute of Art, Baltimore
Relations, Los Angeles Center for Photographic Studies
America: Another Perspective, New York University

1985
Analysis and Passion: Photography Engages Social and Political Issues, Eye Gallery, San Francisco

1984
Family Pictures and Stories, Multi-Cultural Galleries, San Diego

Selected Bibliography

Benner, Susan. "A Conversation with Carrie Mae Weems," *Artweek,* May 7, 1992.

Johnson, Ken. "Generational Saga," *Art in America,* June 1991.

Jones, Kellie. "In Their Own Image," *Artforum,* November 1990.

Kelley, Jeff. "The Isms Brothers, Carrie Mae Weems at SFAI," *Artweek,* May 7, 1992.

Kimmelman, Michael, "Pleasures and Terrors in Home Photographs," *The New York Times,* September 27, 1991.

Lippard, Lucy R. *Mixed Blessings: New Art in a Multicultural America.* New York: Pantheon, 1990.

Moore, Catriona. "The Art of Political Correctness," *Art & Text* 41 (1992).

Reed, Calvin, "Carrie Mae Weems," *Arts Magazine,* January 1991.

Squires, Carol. "Domestic Blitz: The Modern Cleans House," *Artforum,* October 1991.

Weems, Carrie Mae. "Family Stories," in Brian Wallis, ed. *Blasted Allegories: An Anthology of Writings by Contemporary Artists.* New York: New Museum of Contemporary Art, 1987.

Willis-Thomas, Deborah. *Black Photographers 1940–1988: An Illustrated Bio-Bibliography.* New York: Gardner Press, 1989.

Wilson, Judith and Andrea Miller-Keller. *Carrie Mae Weems/Matrix 115* (exhibition brochure). Hartford, CT: Wadsworth Atheneum, 1991.

PAT WARD WILLIAMS

Born Philadelphia, 1948
BFA, Moore College of Art, Philadelphia, 1982
MFA, Maryland Institute College of Art, Baltimore, 1987

Selected Exhibitions

1992
Discovery and Conquest, Smith College, Northampton, MA
Global Politics, Santa Monica Museum of Art
Bridges and Boundaries: African-Americans and American Jews, Jewish Museum, New York

1991
Identity Crisis, Watts Towers Cultural Arts Center, Los Angeles
Diversity and Ethnicity, Center for Photography, Woodstock, NY

1990
MOVE?, Los Angeles Center for Photographic Studies
*Redeye Gallery, Rhode Island School of Design, Providence
The Decade Show, Museum of Contemporary Hispanic Art, The New Museum of Contemporary Art, The Studio Museum in Harlem, New York
Family Stories, Snug Harbor Cultural Center, New York
Art and Conscience, Center for the Arts and Religion, Wesley Theological Seminary, Washington, DC

1989
Political Varieties, Fayerweather Gallery, University of Virginia, Charlottesville
Loaded, Blue Star Art Space, San Antonio, TX
Constructed Images, Studio Museum in Harlem, New York

1988
Politically Charged, First Street Forum, St. Louis
Ford Foundation Grantees, Eubie Blake Cultural Arts Center, Baltimore

1987
Social/Sexual/Personal: Politics, The Gatehouse, Washington, DC
Race and Representation, Hunter College, New York
Image/Identity, Maryland Art Place, Baltimore

1986
Sweet Land of Liberty, School 33 Art Center, Baltimore

Selected Bibliography

"Racism, Identity, and the Blues Aesthetic," *High Performance,* Winter 1990.

Berger, Maurice. "Rassismus in US-Museen?," *Kunstforum International,* May/June 1991.

Collischan Van Wagner, Judy. "Pat Ward Williams: Personal and Political Observations," *CEPA Journal* 4/1 (1990).

_____. "Pat Ward Williams," *Arts Magazine,* March 1989.

Lippard, Lucy R. *Mixed Blessings: New Art in a Multicultural America.* New York: Pantheon, 1990.

Margulis, Stephen. "Pat Ward Williams at the Fayerweather Gallery," *New Art Examiner,* May 1990.

Roth, Moira and Portia Cobb. "An Interview with Pat Ward Williams," *Afterimage,* January 1989.

Selected Exhibitions on Identity / Liste ausgewählter Ausstellungen zum Thema Identität

Difference: On Representation and Sexuality
Curated by Kate Linker and Jane Weinstock. The New Museum of Contemporary Art, New York, 1984
(catalog)

Between Identity/Politics: A New Art
Gimpel Fils, London, January–March 1986
The Arts Centre, Darlington, Spring 1986;
Gimpel and Weitzenhoffer, New York, June 1986
(catalog)

Identity/Desire: Representing the Body
Collins Gallery, University of Strathclyde, Glasgow, 1986

Race and Representation: Art/Film/Video
Hunter College Art Gallery, New York
January 26–March 6, 1987
(catalog)

The Other Body: Cultural Debate in Contemporary British Photography
Photographic Resource Center, Boston University
August 13–September 27, 1987
(catalog)

Cut/Across
Washington Project for the Arts, Washington, D.C.
June 24–March 5, 1988

Autobiography: In Her Own Image
INTAR Gallery, New York, 1988
(catalog)

Identity, Identities: An Exploration of the Concept of Female Identity in Contemporary Society
Curated by Shirley J. R. Madill. Winnipeg Art Gallery
July 24–September 4, 1988
(catalog)

Personal Document/Cultural Identity: Essays in Photography
University Art Gallery, California State University, Chico
October 13–November 18, 1989
(catalog)

Prisoners of Image: Ethnic and Gender Stereotypes
The Alternative Museum, New York
January 7–March 4, 1989
(catalog)

Magiciens de la terre
Musée National d'art Moderne, Centre Georges Pompidou, and La Grande Halle, La Villette, Paris, 1989
(catalog)

Completing the Circle: Six Artists
Organized by the Asian Heritage Council. Southern Exposure Gallery, San Francisco; Triton Museum of Art, Santa Clara, 1990
(catalog)

The Other Story
Curated by Rasheed Araeen. Hayward Gallery, London, November 1990

The Decade Show: Frameworks of Identity in the 1980s
Museum of Contemporary Hispanic Art, The New Museum of Contemporary Art, The Studio Museum in Harlem
May 12/16/18–August 19, 1990
(catalog)

Disputed Identities
Curated by Rupert Jenkins, Chris Johnson, and Portia Cobb. San Francisco Camerawork, October 18–November 24, 1990; Contemporary Arts Center, New Orleans, March 2–31, 1991; Presentation House Gallery, Vancouver, B.C., May 10–June 16, 1991; California Museum of Photography, Riverside, September 7–October 23, 1991
(catalog)

Presumed Identities
Real Art Ways, Hartford, Connecticut, 1990

Interrogating Identity
Curated by Thomas Sokolowski and Kellie Jones. Grey Art Gallery and Study Center, New York University, March 12–May 18, 1991; Museum of Fine Arts, Boston, August 10–November 3, 1991; Walker Art Center, Minneapolis November 23, 1991–February 23, 1992; Madison Art Center March 14–May 10, 1992; Allen Memorial Art Museum, Oberlin, Ohio, September 18–November 29, 1992
(catalog)

The Politics of Difference: Artists Explore Issues of Identity
Curated by Amelia Jones. University Art Gallery, University of California, Riverside, January 12–March 8, 1992

Caught Between the Sheets
Curated by Suzette S. Min. Los Angeles Photographic Center, July 14–August 16, 1992

Dissent, Difference and the Body Politic
Curated by Simon Watson. The Portland Art Museum Portland, Oregon, August 20–October 18, 1992

University Art Museum Staff

Marla C. Berns, *Director*
Elizabeth A. Brown, *Curator*
Sandra Rushing, *Registrar*
Paul Prince, *Exhibitions Designer*
Corinne Gillet-Horowitz, *Curator of Education*
Brian Parshall, *Curatorial Assistant*
Sharon Major, *Public Relations Coordinator*
Rollin Fortier, *Preparator*
Judy McKee, *Administrative Assistant*
Gary Todd, *Office Manager*